THE UNEQUAL HOMELESS

Routledge
New York and London

THE UNEQUAL HOMELESS
Men on the Streets, Women in Their Place

Joanne Passaro

Published in 1996
by Routledge
29 West 35th Street
New York, NY 10001

Published in
Great Britain by
Routledge
11 New Fetter Lane
London EC4P 4EE

Copyright © 1996 by
Routledge
Printed in the
United States of America
on acid-free paper.

Library of Congress Cataloging-in-Publication-Data

Passaro, Joanne
    The unequal homeless: men on the streets,
    women in their place / by Joanne Passaro
    p. cm.
    ISBN 0-41590902-3 (alk. paper).
    — ISBN 0-415-90903-1 (pbk.: alk. paper)
    1. Homeless persons—New York (N.Y.)
    2. Homeless women—New York (N.Y.)
    3. Homelessness.
    I. Title.
HV4506.N6P37 1996   95-47036
362.5'09747'1—dc20   CIP

ACKNOWLEDGMENTS

For my parents, Vincent J. and Betty Chiaramonte Passaro,
my brothers, Paul V. Passaro and Vincent P. Passaro,
my aunt, Rose J. Neser,
and my nephew, Paul M. Passaro

MANY PEOPLE were of enormous help to me in conducting the research on which this book is based. I would particularly like to thank Marc L. Greenberg of the Interfaith Assembly on Homelessness and Housing; Father John Bucki and Sister Mary Galeone of St. Francis Xavier Church; Katherine Oberlies, an attorney who volunteered at the St. Francis Xavier Welfare Rights Clinic; and Peter Malvan and Janet Driver. I am also grateful to The Aspen Institute, which supported the final year of this research with a generous Non-Profit Sector Research Fund grant, #91–NSRF-9.

Over the years I have been taught, inspired, and encouraged by teachers, colleagues and friends. I would especially like to thank Nadia Abu El-Haj, Patricia Bloodgood, Diane Costa, Wayne L. Cotton, Virginia R. Dominguez, James Ferguson, Richard G. Fox, Ernestine Friedl, Malcolm Gillis, Mary Gustafik, Deborah Gustavsen, Fredric Jameson, Jean Grossarth Kawka,

Harold S. Kudler, Liisa Malkki, Joyce McGowan, George McKenna, Molly Mullin, Barbara Newborg, William M. O'Barr, Naomi Quinn, Judith Ruderman, John P. Scanlon, Clotilde Schlayer, the late David M. Schneider, Irene Silverblatt, Barbara Herrnstein Smith, Carol A. Smith, Carol B. Stack, Claudia Strauss, David Thorstad, Jane Tompkins, Rolph Trouillot, Michael D. Webb, Robert P. Weller, Brackette Williams, and Drexel Woodson.

Claudia Koonz supported, cajoled, pushed, and pulled me through the years of research and much of the writing of this book, and I am happy to finally thank her. Most of the ideas here were fine-tuned in dialogue with her; I am grateful for those years of friendship and conversation.

I have been extremely blessed in my colleagues at the Center for Liberal Studies at Clarkson University. The process of revising this manuscript within the framework of their intellectual support and human warmth was a complete pleasure.

One of my oldest and dearest friends, Regina Kahney, read parts of this manuscript at the last minute during a blizzard; her editor's gaze and her insights were extremely helpful. Anne Williams, too, read the manuscript under hectic conditions soon after her arrival at Clarkson, and I thank her for our discussions and her suggestions. Faye Serio rephotographed all of the figures in this book right as it went to press; I'm grateful for her advice and support.

I am in particular debt to Jim Ferguson for his critical reading of many drafts of this manuscript, often on short notice. Jim's comments and suggestions, generously tempered, were invaluable, as is his support and friendhip. I am also extremely grateful to Naomi Quinn, Carol A. Smith, Fred Jameson, Ernestine Friedl, and Claudia Strauss for their comments, criticism, and encouragement all along the way.

I would also like to thank Max Zutty, Marlie Wasserman, and Alan Weider at Routledge for their advice, patience and support.

CONTENTS

INTRODUCTION

THIS BOOK explores the persistence, as opposed to the occurrence, of homelessness. It shows how cultural expressions of beliefs about gender difference help to perpetuate the homelessness of particular groups of people in New York City.

The people who are persistently homeless in Manhattan are, overwhelmingly, black men. Why? The answer, I found, is that homelessness is not simply an economic predicament, but a cultural and moral location—"homeless" means much more than simply "houseless."[1]

Homeless street people are men and women in gender crisis. For homeless men, this crisis usually relates to the culturally contradictory position they occupy—they are viewed both as hypermasculinized and emasculated. These men appear to be independent of the control of women, family, and society, and thus they are considered dangerous, violent, and aggressive. If they are "nonwhite," racism reinforces and exaggerates these fears. Accompanying these hypermasculinized images are emasculated ones—homeless men are failed *men*, in traditional gender terms, because they are dependent and unable to support themselves.

Homeless women, on the other hand, are seen as the apotheosis of Woman—dependent, vulnerable, frightened. They benefit from traditional gender ideologies because their individual failures are not compounded by gender failure—a dependent, needy woman, after all, is no challenge to dominant beliefs. Homeless women quickly learn that to work their way through the system, from emergency shelter through transitional housing to, ultimately, an apartment—they need to behave in such a way as to appear "worthy." Many, therefore, act meek, don't cause trouble, and are grateful for help while in the sight of shelter officials or others who may decide their fates. The homeless women who don't play this game often find themselves having as few options as men.

For homeless men, there is no similar game to be played. The hegemony of sexist and racialist (Appiah, 1992) political projects helps put the question of the survival of these doubly-stigmatized men on a social and moral back burner. The pervasive belief that "they" are getting what they deserve can lull those of us who are not homeless into inaction, for we are faced with complicated feelings, frustrations, and choices about homelessness, and our empathy can be easily overridden when facing the difficult questions about whom to help, how, and at what cost to us as individuals and as a society. That the homeless men New Yorkers encounter with every step might be "unworthy" helps us to dismiss them and their despair.

Feminist critics of welfare are among those who do not sympathize with the plight of these men. Linda Gordon, for instance, has argued that "welfare is a women's issue" (Gordon, 1994a: 311), meaning that maternalist welfare policies are designed to keep women dependent on a patronizing Uncle Sam. Gordon is right, but viewed from the perspective of homelessness her arguments must be recast. For although women are patronized, they can and do strategize and capitalize on their available options in order to survive. Gordon and Nancy Fraser admit that the grim realities of welfare are "as bad or worse for men" (Fraser and Gordon, 1994), but they and other feminists usually ignore this fact—that poor and homeless men are treated far worse by the welfare system than women are, and often have nothing to strategize with. In arguing that welfare is a women's issue, Gordon assumes that men would not get such treatment. She is right, for in most states men get no treatment at all.[2]

The surest way for a homeless person, man or woman, to survive is to have a child. This is not because of increased cash benefits, for these are relatively minimal, but because "family members" are seen differently, and treated differently, by law and, equally significantly, by custom. Family members, people with dependent children, are cared for under a different entitlement program—Aid to Families with Dependent Children (AFDC)—than are childless adults, who, in New York, are eligible for a program called Home Relief. It is far more difficult to "churn" a family—remove them from AFDC entitlement rolls—than it is to take a single adult off Home Relief. As I discuss in this book, families are generally the only homeless people who stand a chance of moving from the streets to an apartment.

This picture is complicated by the fact that while some homeless people are creating families in order to survive, others are leaving their families for the same reason—survival. Numerous studies have shown that as many as half of all homeless women are fleeing domestic abuse and violence. These women, living in economically tenuous circumstances to begin with, do not have the choices open to more privileged women fleeing domestic violence, and often they must choose between homelessness and continued abuse. A significant proportion of homeless men—at least 20%—have also left their families. Most of these men came to feel that the role of family breadwinner was unbearably restrictive and a rip-off as well—as one man explained, "love lasts only as long as the paycheck." For these men and women, the constraining roles available within the nuclear family were contributing factors to their becoming homeless. But despite such restrictions, having a family is often the only alternative to homelessness.

One of the central arguments in this book is that homelessness is a problem about "home," about the cultural gender imperatives that are created and reinforced by the ideology of the nuclear family. This is ignored in most of the literature on homelessness, which concentrates primarily on the economic phenomenon of *houselessness*. Federal and local social welfare initiatives primarily aim at eradicating *house*lessness, not *home*lessness; the only homeless adults who will be housed are those who return to or recreate normative "homes"—and the gender roles they imply—in order to survive. To understand homelessness, that is, to understand who will *remain* homeless as opposed to who will *become* houseless, we must begin by looking at the gender imperatives, and the racialized inflections of those imperatives, that constitute "home."

NEGOTIATING DISTANCES

I did not anticipate these conclusions when I started fieldwork in the summer of 1990. Because of my own positionalities and politics, I had assumed that I would work among homeless women. Their problems, I thought, were more serious than men's, for in addition to all the other dangers of life on the street they faced the constant threat of rape and other physical assault. When I arrived in New York City in June of 1990, I began to notice that I saw far more men on the streets than women, but even these often dramatic disparities did not, at first, alert to me the existence of a noteworthy problem. It was only when daily observations of significant differences along gender lines began piling up that I thought to pose my first question.

This came on a Sunday as I volunteered, which I did most Sundays, with a team of lawyers and law students at a welfare rights project at the St. Francis Xavier soup kitchen. Each week, from our vantage point on a dais at the entrance to the service area, I counted the people on line. Each week about 1,200 homeless people came for supper, and each week no less than 90% of those people were black men. When I finally asked Father John Bucki and Sister Mary Galeone, the parish administrators, where the women were, Sister Mary was surprised: "I've been here five years and I never thought about it! They must be over in Queens and in Brooklyn in the Tier Twos for families [transitional housing; emergency shelters are Tier One housing]. But it's true, we hardly ever see women, except in the first seating [for elderly and handicapped people in the neighborhood who are not homeless]. I guess they don't need us."

As I learned, Sister Mary was right.[3] And I spent the next three years trying to understand why.

The traditional anthropological methodology—participant observation—is largely unelaborated. But I found that by conceptualizing participation and observation as elements in dialectical tension I had a particularly rich heuristic, one that necessitated attention to multiple perspectives in order to produce adequate social description. I decided that to best answer my questions—"why are most of the homeless street people black men?"; "where are the homeless women?"—I needed to choose sites that would afford me a variety of perspectives along a participant/observer continuum. For instance, I volunteered in a city-run family emergency shelter, working and talking with clients as well as city workers; I joined meetings, demonstrations and social activities with the men from Homeward Bound, a shelter/self-help group run by homeless people themselves; I worked at the weekly welfare rights clinic run at the St. Francis Xavier soup kitchen; I volunteered at the Interfaith Assembly on Homelessness and Housing, a nonprofit advocacy and aid organization; and I interned, researched, and wrote articles for *City Limits*, a progressive magazine that served as a watchdog for housing/community issues in city and state government. These sites were not the only positions I interacted and observed from, and I did not spend equal amounts of time in all of them. They were, however, the scaffolding around which I organized the rest of my activities—interviewing panhandlers; joining in or watching demonstrations; going to meetings of neighborhood housing organizations and of architects and other groups interested in addressing homelessness; discussing books and attending films and plays with homeless people; playing cards; spending days in the 42nd Street library; and sitting in Central Park or one of the numerous other parks and street locations where homeless people congregated.

I had many doubts and fears as I began research. I already knew what the Urban Institute reported in 1988, that "the homeless are disproportionately black and Hispanic, more so than are the poor generally" (1988: 1). Would my "whiteness" mark any effort I made as patronizing? Would I be met with hostility? Would my attempt to gather material to write a dissertation, and advance through graduate school and presumably up the class ladder, necessarily oppress and diminish the people I was working with?

These doubts were initially paralyzing. I spent the first few days in New York assessing possible field sites and volunteer opportunities, reading, thinking, and generally avoiding homeless people. But finally I mustered enough courage to walk, with my heart in my throat, into Father Demo Square, a nearby park on Sixth Avenue where homeless people slept at night and hung out during the day. I walked to a bench and sat down to read the paper, and eventually looked up and said hello to the man sitting next to me.

In one very important sense, the difficulties of my fieldwork were all downhill from there. My field experiences over the next three years were in general characterized by the surprising openness and lack of hostility of my homeless informants. I found what Nancy Scheper-Hughes (1992) so movingly desrcibed in her own research, that most people welcomed the chance to talk, to be heard, to feel that their experiences held significance for others. I shared joy and pain and love and fear and the whole gamut of human emotions with homeless people, and I would contend that I neither oppressed nor harmed any of them, not the ones I came to know well nor the ones I saw only once, like Hector, my companion on the bench that first day in Demo Square.

I spoke with well over 1,000 homeless people in the years of my research. My initial year of fieldwork began in June of 1990 and continued through August of 1991. I then conducted follow-up studies over the next two years, ending in May of 1993. I formally interviewed, for periods ranging from twenty minutes to about two hours, 380 homeless people—202 men and 178 women. Many of the interviews took place over lunch or another meal, for which I paid, and in some cases I paid $20 for interviews of two hours or more. These encounters were among the richest, most heart-wrenching and rewarding experiences I have ever had, for the intensity of homeless people's needs for practical support and human kindness helped break the barriers of strangeness and reticence that often accompany first meetings. I always found the courage of homeless men and women inspiring and exhilarating, and I left many encounters vowing never again to let myself be depressed when I was, after all, so lucky. That vow was broken almost as frequently as it was made, of course, but a profound sense of wonder at having touched and been touched by so many lives remains.

Like any New Yorker, my daily life in the city required that I navigate many complex series of encounters and negotiate often enormous social differences.

5

But the social distances that were most difficult to overcome were not neces-sarily those that existed between me and homeless people.

In the spring of 1991, literary agent Charlotte Sheedy introduced me to Lane Montgomery, a screenwriter who was working on a script about home-lessness. When Lane heard that I was in school at Duke, she asked, "Oh, do you know Angie?." I thought she was referring to one of her daughters, but the "Angie" in question turned out to be the late Ambassador Angier Biddle Duke, whom I had never met and under usual circumstances would never be in the position to meet. A few weeks later, though, I did meet Ambassador Duke for breakfast at his home at River House. We had a long and lively con-versation about mutual interests and experiences in Central America and Eastern Europe, and, at the end of the meal, Ambassador Duke invited me to return later that afternoon, "for cocktails with Shevardnadze."

I had various research activities planned for that day, so I walked the sixty or so blocks south from River House both to dissipate my disbelief and to get some of those tasks done. At that time I was studying the ways homeless peo-ple were being hustled off expensive shopping streets, so I canvassed the avenues talking to police, store owners and homeless vendors and panhandlers. I then tried to arrange a follow-up interview with Jean, a homeless woman who traveled into New York every day from Jersey City to panhandle. The thoughts and feelings I had about Jean were typical of my reactions among homeless people— there but for a couple of breaks go I. Like Jean, I had come from a working class New York family; like Jean I had often been marginally employed before returning to undergraduate school; like Jean I had gone back to college because of the need to earn a living wage. But unlike Jean, I was going to meet Soviet politician Edward Schevardnadze in three hours.

Most people assume that I had to negotiate chasms of social difference in working with homeless people, but I found that while those differences exist-ed, they were not as dramatic as those I encountered with people of the other extreme. For instance, in preparing for my return to Ambassador Duke's home that day, I realized that the neat-but-casual clothes I had worn for breakfast were both the best clothes I had and also totally inappropriate for cocktails. After an hour of panic I placed an emergency call to Charlotte Sheedy, who graciously offered to lend me a handpainted blazer and a flowing black skirt for the event. I felt odd in someone else's skin, a point driven home in the ele-vator at Ambassador Duke's when another guest admired the jacket and asked who had designed it.

In contrast, I never had to borrow clothes, or even "dress down," to work among homeless people. However, these visits to Ambassador Duke's apartment, like those to the opera or to any of the expensive restaurants or other events I attended, were not occasions where I "left the field"—that such extremes of privilege and devastation coexist in such close quarters in New York City is not coincidence, and elites were as much a part of my analysis as homeless people were.

But while assumptions—my own and others'—about to whom I would feel "other" were off the mark, in many important ways I did have more in common with New York elites than with homeless people. I was a graduate student at a pretigious academic institution, and my chances for survival, and even relative prosperity, were good. Suprisingly, I found that it was not only my similarities to homeless New Yorkers but also this social distance from them that enabled my work.

THE LUXURY OF EMPATHY

One of my first volunteer experiences was at a city-run family shelter.[4] The first thing I noticed as I walked down the halls of the shelter was a big, hand-lettered sign posted outside the door of the social services office:

> Unless you are called to office you will not see a case worker. Period. All complaints will be managed by Housekeeping.

Housekeeping? These people must be swamped, I thought, and later that day I went to investigate. Because I was a volunteer, not a resident, I was permitted to open office doors and walk in, unannounced and uninvited. It was 3:30 in the afternoon, and in that social services office five people sat at their desks. Every one of them was reading a New York tabloid newspaper, either the *Post* or the *News*. I thought then that this must be breaktime; it was not. Later I was told by one of the shelter's staff, "Fucking off is the norm. Working's the exception. Not just here, in this department. It's the whole city."

My first assignment as a volunteer at the shelter was to find words for a spelling bee for children of three age groups, 3rd and 4th grades, 5th and 6th grades, and 7th and 8th grades. I had to find fifty words for each group, and I wondered aloud what a "third grade word" was. My supervisor, the one who had just given me the assignment, said, "Oh, just use three-letter words for the first group, then four and five letter words for the older kids." "C-a-t for third graders? No way!," I said, "I think I'll go look in the library." "It's locked," she said, "I'll get someone to open it." When I wondered why the library would be locked, the supervisor responded: "We don't have anyone who wants to sit there."

So I went to the library, which, once unlocked, yielded a trove of out-of-date textbooks that perfectly suited my purpose. I came back an hour later with three lists of words, all written in my best printing, none of which contained a three- or even four-letter word. "Finished already?," the supervisor asked. "That was the only task I had for you for the week!"

With time on my hands I went to the recreation room, where kids who were not in school for one reason or another were sitting. The workers had given them a task—to write a story about Halloween—but most of the kids were doing something else, and the few who were still writing needed help. The two shelter employees in the room stayed at the entrance desk, talking and reading the paper. I had not been given any directives; I had to decide for myself whether to help the kids or ignore them.

That first afternoon I felt awkward and uncomfortable, unsure how the kids would respond to me and how much hostility would be aimed at the only white person in the room, the one who was trying to "help." The six children I worked with that day were shy, but they didn't seem to mind the attention. I wondered, though, whether my efforts were just another in the series of indignities that homeless people experience daily.

The next day I had my answer: the kids, with eight-year-old Kareem and his sister Sophia leading the pack, ran to meet me; they all remembered my name and clamored for attention and help and praise. I was incredibly moved—after six weeks in Manhattan trying to fathom homelessness, I had already deleted joy from my list of possibilities for human interaction.

During the painful and depressing October at that shelter, at least half of my time was spent helping the kids with their homework or with the make-work they were given to keep them still. I wondered why I was the only one who helped them; surely, I thought, it's not because I'm the only nice person here. I began to understand the situation when I realized that despite the fact that many shelter workers had master's degrees, the initials of which they displayed prominently and even appended to the end of their names in routine memos, I seemed to be the only one who knew what a homonym was, or an intransitive verb, or a metaphor.

A few days later an African-American man living at the shelter, discussing the bad treatment he and his family received at the hands of shelter employees, complained, "These niggers, man, act like they ass ain't black. They see me, put on airs, and they come from the same damn block I do. The same block."

This man's statement recalled sections of Bourdieu's *Distinction* (1984), and it made both the attitude of shelter workers and the way they wore their college degrees on their sleeves intelligible. Many of these employees, I realized, were in a peculiar position of power over people who came from similar age groups, class backgrounds and often even high schools and neighborhoods. But despite their college educations they seemed surprisingly unqualified; those memos were rife with misspellings and nonsentences. Often I recorded in my field notes that many clients seemed to have more on the ball than the workers. And perhaps that was the point: the city workers and the shelter clients belonged to the same employment pool. The workers' position was perhaps too precarious to afford empathy; they spent much of their energy distancing themselves from clients instead of forming potentially identity-threatening relationships with them. During that fall of 1990 the talk in the city was all about budget cuts, and many of these workers were afraid of losing their jobs. This did not seem to inspire, as one might think, renewed effort; it only seemed to entrench their hostility towards what some called the "lazy, good for nothing" homeless people. Ironically, in seeking to draw distinctions between themselves and the people who lived in the shelter, city workers displayed those same negative qualities they used to describe their clients. At times it seemed that the only difference between homeless and nonhomeless people in that shelter was that one group had a tenuous hold on a decent city job.

The few nonhomeless people in the shelter who seemed able to afford empathy were people who stood totally outside the struggle for survival: Edith, a Board of Education worker with tenure, and I, a poor but privileged graduate student from Duke. This conclusion, that empathy is often a luxury, haunted me, for we were in the midst of a global recession, and I had already noticed a resurgence of ethnic and racial hatred in the city. And given the incompetence and ill-will with which the massive New York welfare bureaucracy often operated, a situation that anthropologist Anna Lou DeHavenon (1989–90) described as "Charles Dickens meets Franz Kafka," I doubted that there was much room in the system for human kindness.

Battles over boundaries, with self-preservation as the putative stakes, were common at the shelter, and, almost invariably, homeless people were the losers. But the combatants were not always the tenuously employed. Since first walking down those halls I had been passing a locked "computer room" to which a number of new machines had recently been donated. I had been looking forward to organizing classes for interested residents, since word processing was one of my few marketable skills. But after noticing that the room remained locked day after day, I finally asked a shelter employee about it.

"Oh, it's been shut since the computers got here, and it will probably stay shut…it's a turf war. The Board of Ed wants jurisdiction and so does HRA [the Human Resources Administration, which oversees the distribution of public assistance in New York City]. Nobody uses it until the bigwigs decide who it belongs to."

And nobody did decide, at least during the four weeks I was there.

After I made plans to spend November working in a private homeless self-help shelter, I confessed my frustrations to Ellie, a woman who had worked at the shelter for a number of years. "This place is such a zoo, people can't stand it," she said. "There's not a lot of room for real work, though there's need galore." I asked Ellie about the library—why it was locked up practically all day, when it was the only room in the entire building that had decent lighting and when clients kept requesting access to it so they could read or fill out forms. "Nobody gives a flying shit about these people, and maybe more than that…keeping the library open would be a do-nothing job, sitting at a desk.

That's all people do here anyway, read the paper, pick their nose. But better to read the paper alone than to be helping people while doing it."

"How can so many poorly trained, apathetic people be working for the City?" I later asked two other employees. One, a supervisor, said, "For instance, I would never hire you, Ms. Passaro. I'm sorry to say. I would never hire anybody who could do my job as well as me. If I hire you, you might have my job inside a month. I hate to say it, but I have a home and a family to support....Did you ever hear the phrase 'the As hire the Bs'? Well, the As hire the Bs, the Bs hire the Cs, and now in the city it's the Fs hiring Zs."

The other City employee, discussing impending budget cuts and feared layoffs, said, "I'd be willing to bet that if they fired 80% of us, we'd get just as much work done. Maybe more, because morale would be better. Right now, if you do your job right—which it's important for me to do because of my recovery program, the need for self-respect—I have to be careful not to seem like a hot-dogger because I only take hour lunches or, if I take longer, I stay later at the end of the day. But I have to do it [actually work 40 hours a week] unobtrusively."

This was indeed a page out of Kafka, having to hide evidence of the fact that you were doing your job for fear of losing it. I knew that my experiences in this shelter were not exceptional, but I fought hard to avoid the conclusion that they were the rule. I was not usually successful.

RETHINKING GENDER AND "FAMILIES"

One of the enduring lessons from my experiences in that shelter was a good one to learn early in my fieldwork; it was also a humbling one to an academic who specializes in the social construction of identities. I had learned how situational the content of any given identity was (cf. Dominguez, 1989) and I was also aware that the boundaries of identity were permeable (Barth, 1969). But though these understandings from my earliest graduate student days were central to the course of study and research I subsequently followed, I nonetheless found I that I did not always act on them.

While navigating the streets and alleys of the city, I became guarded and tense if I found myself alone with a man, but I relaxed if the only person nearby was a woman. Walking up and down the stairwells and hallways of the shelter proved my folly; most of the unnecessary jostling I received was from women, and they were nearly as likely as men to stage drunken brawls and pull weapons. One inhabitannt, Rosa, who had arrived at the shelter a few weeks earlier, explained her experiences with other women in the shelter: "Here the women aren't women anymore … they spread feces all over. They aren't females. You're in trouble here even if you don't mix with them."

Rosa's interpretation was based on traditional ideas about what "men" and "women" are like; the "women" who weren't women anymore were those who had crossed the normative boundaries of gender identity by exhibiting anger, violence, and a disregard for public hygiene. For me, Rosa's story served as a reminder of the extraordinary coercive power of gender: to deny the traditional limits of gender—to act in such a way as to be open to the charge of being "no longer a woman" or "not a real man"—is a social transgression, and the consequences can be enormous. It is an especially risky practice for homeless men and women, people who are extremely vulnerable and dependent on public support. In general, the homeless people who are most likely to get help are those who appear to be exemplars of traditional gender ideals.

Gender, like race, is a category of oppression; it is a taxonomic tool of systems of domination and subordination. In recent discussions, feminists have moved beyond dualistic notions of gender as foundational "identity" to focus instead on the multivalent and hybridized performative aspects of gender (Butler, 1990; Garber, 1992). The focus on performance is an effort to better comprehend the variety of ways we each are engendered and engender ourselves, and to better see and understand the ways that race and class are interwoven into the variety of gender positions open to us.[5]

Conceptualizing gender as performance, as opposed to identity, is a powerful analytic stance, one that is capable of capturing the contextuality and ephemerality of the many gendered acts any subject performs. But in the multiplicity of theoretical possibilities that have emerged, the fact that gender is a mandatory performance is sometimes submerged. Each of us may choose, at different times and in different contexts, from among the performative dances of gender that are available and apprehensible to us, but dance we must.

This coercion is particularly clear in the experiences of homeless men and women, whose choices are severely constrained and whose very survival depends on the sympathy and support of government employees and the general public. Homeless women, if they are to survive, must typically perform the dance of the dutiful dependent. Homeless men have fewer options; if their skin is relatively light ("white"), they might find someone in a public or private agency to "take a chance" on them. More often, however, the only performance available to men is the role of street person. One of the few possibilities homeless men have of escaping the streets is to become a family member—to father a child. This child can then be used as leverage for moving in with the mother if she is housed, or, if she is not, to then apply with her and the child for the special benefits that accrue to families. In other words, efforts to protect children also endanger children, because having children gives homeless adults one of their best chances of survival. This social calculus is not lost on homeless people.

The celestialization of families persists despite demographic trends indicating that more and more people are creating affiliative ties outside of marriage, cohabitation and childrearing. For even as increasing numbers of adults are choosing to live alone or outside of traditional nuclear family arrangements—the 1990 U.S. census found that nearly 23 million Americans now live alone, including 11% of all 35–44 year-olds[6]—a family values agenda is currently gaining momentum in the United States. The contemporary family values movement appears to have at least two strands. One of these is a general conviction that the market should not rule all domains of life, that social relations of obligation and responsibility should not be reduced to consumer choice. The more attention-grabbing sector of the movement is the extreme right, whose antigay, antiabortion forces aim at reinforcing what they perceive as weakening gender and nuclear family imperatives. Opposition to the implications of a family values agenda, and a battle to control that agenda, are evident in figures 1.1 and 1.2. Figure 1.1 was posted all over the streets of lower Manhattan during the 1992 Presidential election season; entitled "Traditional Family Values," it depicts a group in KKK regalia. This poster is a response to the extreme right, whose "family values" often euphemize virulent racism. Figure 1.2, declaring that "Hate is Not a Family Value," is a bumper sticker that has become popular over the past several years; it is an effort to extricate family values from a platform of hate. As these figures suggest, the stakes in the "family values" battles can be nothing less than survival for anyone who deviates from the cultural ideals of sexuality, race and gender. This is particularly true for homeless people.

12

Throughout this work, and particularly in the next chapter, *House and Home*, I argue that what is often referred to as a symptom of psychological or social dysfunction among homeless people—their "disaffiliation" and disaffection with dominant institutions— exists among the rest of us as well, if two of those "supportive institutions" are marriage and the nuclear family. Disaffiliation from nuclear families can be reconceptualized as an active and thoughtful choice rather than a "missed opportunity"; as a decision to leave a pathological situation rather than as a pathological decision. This is often difficult to see when working with homeless people, because the price of those choices is so high. But for housed people who choose to disaffiliate with normative gender roles, and/or the heterosexual and nuclear family imperatives, that high price is often paid in other ways.

In the chapters that follow, the stories and words of the homeless people you will encounter have been minimally edited for clarity. I have tried to preserve, as much as possible, the integrity of individual voices while avoiding caricaturing them.

In Chapter Three, *Beyond the Panopticon*, I explore the ways in which traditional definitions of manhood and masculinity undercut poor, black, and homeless men. I present the experiences of homeless men who feel that

Figure 1.1

Figure 1.2

breadwinner expectations and the economics of traditional nuclear families undermined their chances for self-fulfillment and were relevant to their homelessness. For these men, being "successful" men meant being constrained as human beings. On the other hand, I also explore the ways that race and poverty have prevented other men from ever living up to traditional notions of masculine success, and how their homelessness was, in many ways, overdetermined. For all of these men, once they become homeless, for whatever reason, there was, and is, little chance of ever getting off the streets.

Chapter Four, "*Sex or Survival*," is an analysis of the contradictions of gender in the lives of homeless women. While many of these women have fled domestic abuse and violence at home, they find that they can survive, and will be housed, as long as they embody traditional ideals of womanhood—docility and dependence. The reinscription of these gender imperatives is the price of survival for homeless women, and though most of them eventually agree to pay it, many are aware of the costs.

In Chapter Five, *Imagined Immunities*, I present a semiotics of public space in New York, the human geography sculpted out of prevailing gender ideologies and homeless men and women's differential opportunities for survival. In neighborhood NIMBY ("Not in my Backyard") campaigns, social policy and precedent, media coverage, and the sympathies of New Yorkers, homeless women and families are given opportunities that men are not. But in order to survive, homeless women have little choice but to be active agents of their own suburbanization, complicit in a system that defines their place at "home" and that subsidizes homes for them in the outer boroughs beyond the borders of Manhattan. The struggle over Manhattan public space is left largely to homeless black men, who are left without homes in part because of prevailing beliefs that they don't "belong" at home, or, by extension, in society, without the domesticating influences of women and children.

I conclude this book by arguing that feminism can no longer leave men at the margins of its analyses; that social welfare programs must treat all adults equally, childless or not; and that the affirmative action programs of the next century might work best by addressing class—as opposed to race and gender—inequities. Continuing to differentiate people in terms of race and gender only perpetuates the salience of those categories and the discrimination they entail, obscuring the processes through which people come to share unequally in political and economic power.

HOUSE AND HOME

chapter 2

WHO ARE THE HOMELESS?

I

Citizens of the United States enjoy no federal legal right to shelter; this right has been established at the state level in California and West Virginia and at the municipal level in Washington, D.C., New York City, Saint Louis, and Atlantic City.[1] According to most estimates[2], there are anywhere from one to three million homeless people in the United States.

Who are these unsheltered people? Why do we call them "homeless" instead of "houseless?" How does the homeless population in New York City compare with homeless populations across the country?

If all demographics convey at best partial truths, counts of homeless people convey still less. The estimates I found of the homeless population in New York City ranged from 30,000 to 100,000; homeless advocacy organizations in general espoused figures towards the high end,[3] while New York City's federally mandated Comprehensive Homeless Assistance Plan spanned both poles, estimating that at any given point in time 35,000 to 90,000 people are homeless in the City. The 1990 U.S. Census supported the lower estimates; their figures, and the classifications they used, appear in Table 2.1.

Because of my interest in the relevance of race to homelessness as well as my more general focus on the processes and products of social classification, I paid particular attention to the taxonomic criteria used to present population figures. As is evident in Table 2.1, the Census Bureau divides the general population, as well as the homeless population, into various "races" and "Hispanic origin," which, for the first time in a U.S. Census, is not considered a racial category.

Table 2.1

1990 Census population characteristics of New York City, including totals of homeless people living in shelters and visible in street locations[†]

Borough	White	Black	Amer. Indian, Eskimo Aluet	Asian/Pacific Islander	Hispanic origin	White, not Hispanic origin
BRONX						
Total Pop.	430,077	449,399	6,069	35,562	523,111	273,503
Homeless						
Shelters	283	1,800	26	5	1,176	151
Streets	138	945	4	15	513	72
BROOKLYN						
Total Pop.	1,078,549	872,305	7,969	111,251	462,411	923,229
Homeless						
Shelters	510	4,059	45	33	1,353	259
Streets	474	1,669	3	15	499	396
MANHANTTAN						
Total Pop.	867,227	326,967	5,728	110,629	386,630	726,755
Homeless						
Shelters	3,352	7,176	106	181	3,436	2,582
Streets	1,564	4,020	30	109	2,470	880
QUEENS						
Total Pop.	1,129,192	423,211	7,050	238,336	381,120	937,557
Homeless						
Shelters	394	1,966	20	9	813	221
Streets	172	441	4	16	155	116
STATEN ISLAND						
Total Pop.	322,043	30,630	715	16,941	30,239	303,081
Homeless						
Shelters	66	310	0	3	110	42
Streets	19	42	1	0	9	17

[†]Census of Population, General Population Characteristics, New York, Table 64

16

But how many "races" are presented? Along with "White," "Black," "American Indian, Eskimo or Aleut," and "Asian or Pacific Islander," there exists a residual classification, "White, not of Hispanic origin." Is this a race, or is the uninflected "White" the race? And why is there no parallel category, "Black, not of Hispanic origin?" If the Census Bureau were trying to determine racial differences among people of Hispanic origin, it would have been necessary to include it. But I think that these classifications reveal a different task, an attempt to distill out "pure" whiteness.[4]

As new Census publications were released in subsequent months, the trend to delineate racial differences—and reaffirm race difference—continued, with particular emphasis on distinguishing between Hispanic origin whites and other whites. Of the 83 tables, for instance, in the 2-volume *General Population Characteristics, New York*,[5] twenty-two deal with "Race and Hispanic origin," two with "White persons," two with "White, not Hispanic origin persons and households," five with "Hispanic origin persons and households," and two with "Black persons and households." Throughout these tables and other Census publications, the care taken to differentiate characteristics of "Hispanic persons" from other "White persons" seems to indicate a reluctance to relinquish an Hispanic racial category; whites of Hispanic origin do not get to mix among other whites for long.

But given this concern with racial purity, it is noteworthy that the process of determining pure "blackness" is missing. This is, I suggest, because such a task is inconceivable in contemporary U.S. culture, for "pure blackness" is oxymoronic. The process of distilling pure whiteness can only be made sensible given the pervasive beliefs about race which are, as I will argue throughout this work, central to understanding how and why homelessness persists among particular groups of people. "Racial thinking" is a social problem at two levels—in terms of the particular contents ascribed to certain racial categories by dominant ideologies, and in the very operation of defining and classifying people according to putative race. As long as we put so much effort into discriminating types of people by race and whiteness, can we fail to discriminate against them in terms of our evaluations of their intrinsic human or social worth?

One especially telling example of how racism can perpetuate inaction on the problems of homelessness in the United States occurred on the international stage. In 1990, the staff of the U.S. Commission on Security and Cooperation in Europe had to confront charges made in the United Nations that the United States was not in compliance with the international Helsinki Human Rights Accords of 1975 because of its failure to adequately address the homelessness crisis. The United States was considered in violation of the Accords because it provided "insufficient supplies of publicly financed housing to meet the needs of economically disadvantaged citizens" (1990: 2). The U.S. Commission acknowledged the problem, and admitted that racial minorities were disproportionately represented among the homeless:

> The Fair Housing Act, a part of the Civil Rights Act of 1968, prohibits discrimination in the sale, rental or financing of housing and requires HUD [the U.S. Department of Housing and Urban Development] and the Justice Department to enforce such provisions. Despite the existence of this legislation, Census data and field tests indicate continued discrimination against blacks and hispanics in the housing market, a high level of segregation in all American cities with sizable minority populations, and a resulting limited access to affordable housing. In 1985, HUD estimated that an average of two million instances of discrimination occur each year. Such discrimination can significantly diminish housing options for minorities in general, and low-income minorities in particular (1990: 17).

Despite this admission, or perhaps because of it, the report ends with a striking call to inaction:

> Privatism and localism have traditionally guided social welfare in America. The Nation's response to the problem of homelessness—the joining of public and private forces to assist those in need—is in the best tradition of American problem solving....Those entities which have been providing assistance to the homeless, including local governments, private voluntary agencies, and, recently, many States, should continue to be the primary vehicles for delivering assistance (ibid: 68).

In other words, while the U.S. government acknowledged the interconnectedness of racism and homelessness, it also washed its hands of the problem, passing the buck to charities and local governments, "in the best tradition of American problem solving."

II

In stark contrast to the proliferation of data about the race of homeless people and of the general population, the gender of homeless people, though recorded by census enumerators, was not computed and is not published by the Census Bureau. Upon inquiring how I might obtain access to that information, I was initially informed that I would have to pay the New York Data Center in Albany to tabulate the homelessness figures in New York by gender. However, early in that process a Data Center employee put me in contact with the New York Department of City Planning, which had already requested the same tabulation. Those figures, which cover only the Borough of Manhattan, are listed in table 2.2.[6]

Table 2.2

1990 Population Figures for Homeless People by Gender in Manhanttan[†]

	Male	Female
Visble in street locations	7823	2624
In shelters	13548	9161

†Source: The New York Department of City Planning

As Table 2.2 indicates, there are far more men on the streets than women. This, I think, is attributable to two factors: a design flaw in Census methodology, and the differential options available to homeless women and men.

The Census Bureau's effort to count homeless people, "Shelter and Street Night" (commonly known as S-Night), was an approximately ten to twelve-hour operation nationwide, beginning at 6 p.m. on March 20, 1990 and continuing through the early morning hours of March 21.[7] Most, if not all, of these hours were, at least in New York, dark and cold. As I discuss in chapter five, many of the women who panhandle on the streets of Manhattan during the day leave the city for the suburbs at night, where they either live in shelters or find safer street locations. The sheltered women would not be counted on the streets, even if they spent their days there. This problem is related to the second factor relevant to lower numbers of women on the streets— the better options women have because of a dominant maternalist and protectionist ideology in which they are viewed as dependent, worthier, and/or more easily "rehabilitatable" than men. The results of the convergence of these two factors is a reinscription of "women's place" in a gendered private realm. Homeless men's struggles for survival largely occur in public Manhattan streets, while women's struggles are less visible, usually occurring within the walls of transitional housing in the outer boroughs, particularly Brooklyn and Queens.

Table 2.2 also indicates that there is less disparity in the numbers of women and men in city shelters than on the streets. But these numbers, too, require unpacking. The New York Human Resources Administration (HRA) compiles records of nightly shelter utilization and monthly averages. For March 7, 1990, for instance (a night that Alka Gupta of the HRA called an especially big night for singles), there were 7,993 single men and 1,458 single women housed in City shelters throughout the five boroughs; 1,226 homeless families housed in hotels; 563 housed in Tier 1 emergency shelters; and 1,914 in Tier 2 shelters, for a total of 3,703 families.

19

Ms. Gupta supports what homelessness researchers (e.g., Reyes and Waxman, 1989 and Burt and Cohen, 1988) have concluded: that the vast majority of these homeless families consist of women and children. This is not immediately evident in H.R.A. figures, which list over 5,000 adults within the 3,703 families; since adults in families also include children over the age of 18, the presence of more than one adult per family does not necessarily indicate a two-parent family. On the night of March 7, of the 21,199 persons in City-run shelters, 9,501 were single men and women; the majority of people sheltered that night were family members—women and their male or female children. This is invisible in Table 2.2, which includes children.

But these statistics do not indicate as much as would a comparison of the numbers of family members vs. single people who have been moved out of the shelter system entirely and into subsidized apartments. Across the nation, the overwhelming majority of housing stock available to homeless people has historically gone and continues to go to homeless families. New York City is no exception. The New York Housing Authority, for example, has housed thousands of homeless people since fiscal year 1988–89. That year, 1,747 apartments were made available to homeless people; in 1989-90, 2,408 apartments; in 1990-91, 1,557 apartments; in 1991-92, 1,405 apartments; and for the period July 1–November 30, 1992, 622 apartments. An NYHA official acknowledged that "well over 95%" of these apartments (and perhaps up to 97 or 98%) went to families. Some private organizations share this family-centered approach. Andrew Cuomo's project HELP (Housing Enterprise for the Less Privileged), for instance, also concentrates on helping homeless families. The HELP rationale is similar to the City's: as a HELP vice-president explained, "families give each other more support, so they are better risks." Single adults (i.e., people without children) need more help, so they get less. Children are often not well served by this focus on family members, since too many of them are being born to give adults access to family privileges.

The results of a family-based approach to homelessness are clear on the streets. In early 1990, four homeless research assistants and I surveyed 500 homeless people we randomly encountered in the daylight on the streets, trying to assess the length of homelessness among particular groups of people. We found that the 302 childless men in the survey reported being homeless for an average of 42 months. In contrast, the 74 childless women we surveyed had been homeless for 27 months; 116 women with children for 12 months; and 8 men with children for 10 months.[8]

Even liberal activists have left unchallenged the trend to discriminate against childless adults. The monthly housing and community activist magazine *City Limits*, for example, published a graph in each issue indicating changes in monthly numbers of homeless families; when I asked the editor, Doug Zaretsky, why the family was the unit of analysis, he cited "the empathy factor," arguing that focusing on families was the only way to get his audience to care about the problem of homelessness. And the Urban Institute was able to conclude that, "On the good side, this survey [Burt and Cohen, 1988] reveals that while there are families among the homeless who use the shelters and the soup kitchens, these families represent only a small percentage of that population. Moreover, in almost all respects homeless families are less destitute than are their single homeless counterparts" (Urban Institute 1988: 1).

This is the kind of information that is usually lost in statistical or economic studies on homelessness, which because of their broad focus can neither depict nor account for the persistence of homelessness, as opposed to its occurrence. Nor can they help us understand the ways race, gender, and family values operate as criteria of social worth and how chronic *homelessness* is the ultimate expression of these equations.

THE ECONOMICS OF HOUSELESSNESS

> What distinguishes the fine studies of contemporary homelessness that began to emerge in the mid-1980s from most of the studies that appeared between 1880 and 1980 is the emphasis on the homeless condition rather than on the homeless per se. (Barak, 1991: 21)

The studies that Gregg Barak alludes to above, those that emphasize the structural causes of homlessness, are best described as dealing with the phenomenon of *houselessness*. In this section I will briefly sketch these analyses of the global, local, and personal economic changes that have led to the displacement of millions of human beings in the United States since 1980.

Most current scholarship distinguishes its object of study—homelessness—from work in the past about hoboes and vagabonds (e.g., Anderson, 1924). Great pains are taken to distinguish the so-called "new" or "heterogeneous" homeless from what is characterized as the "traditional," almost quaint, Skid Row resident of the past.[9]

In one sense, the "new" vs. "old" dichotomy can be seen as coming to terms with the differences implied by *homeless* vs. *houseless*—vagabonds of old could be viewed as "homeless" in the sense that the traditional[10] view of them was as individuals who preferred to ride the rails rather than have normative home lives. The recent literature primarily describes what I am calling here *houselessness*, the changes in world and local economies that in the 1980s led to unprecedented numbers of men, women, and children living in parks, abandoned buildings, overcrowded city shelters, or on the streets atop subway grates.

People writing within this "new" genre have generally and emphatically rejected the earlier culture of poverty position that (mis)characterized the work of a number of theorists of the second wave of urban anthropology.[11]

21

These theorists, such as Oscar Lewis (1968), Ulf Hannerz (1969), and James Spradley (1970), worked within a modernization theory framework that focused on values. Urban ghettos were often studied with the assumption that they were relatively autonomous from mainstream society, but that their values somehow reflected (though in a skewed fashion) those of the larger society. Culture was both a relatively stable phenomenon as well one that was produced by elites. The work of some of these theorists was used in ways they never intended, and to draw conclusions they themselves decried: that the "cultures" of poverty were essentially noncultures, and that to move from poverty to plenty required a change in values, the adoption of "Culture." Poverty-ravaged groups, often described today as "underclasses,"[12] could neither make nor transform culture since, by definition, they lived outside it. All they could do was adopt it, and thereby become "worthy."

This view, that poor or homeless people deserve their fates, is still common today. The goal of countering this conclusion is an important one, and this has been a primary aim of the new homelessness (or what I am calling houselessness) literature, which identifies the international, national, and local economic changes since 1980 as the basis of homelessness in the United States. There is no doubt that the massive defunding of federal housing programs that took place in the 1980s (an astounding 80% decrease, from $30 billion in 1980 to $6 billion in 1990[13]) is the economic basis of most homelessness today. But one of the consequences of this approach, which focuses on the economic causes of homelessness and generally avoids cultural explanations that might lead to charges of blaming the victims, is that the consciousness and agency of homeless people are largely absent from the literature. Homeless people are still victims, though now blameless.

Many recent studies use analyses similar to that of David Harvey (1989) to explain particular changes in the nature of capitalism and to underscore the urgency, and the scope, of the action needed to reverse the trends.

Harvey (1989) argued that the capitalist world has undergone a new round of "time-space compression" since the 1960s, marked by the ease of satellite communication and declining transportation costs. This global compression increased the flexibility of capital, allowing decisions to be implemented almost immediately anywhere around the world. Capital's power was enhanced, unsurprisingly, at the expense of workers and organized labor. One important effect of this change from a multinational to a truly global capitalism has been a widespread reconstitution of the labor system, in particular an increasing reliance on and institutionalization of a two-tiered labor system. This system consists of a core of full-time, permanent workers with job security and benefits, and a periphery of two sub-groups: relatively interchangeable full-time workers with readily available skills (such as secretaries, clerical workers, and less-skilled manual workers), and part-time or casual laborers. To remain even peripherally employed, these laborers must themselves be increasingly flexible in terms of their skills, their geographic location, and their willingness to work without benefits or job security. Harvey's analysis indicates that the peripheral categories have grown significantly in the last few years, and it predicts that the gulf separating core and periphery within as well as across nations will continue to widen (1989: 141-172).

And indeed, six years later, we have seen ample evidence that Harvey was right. On April 17, 1995, new studies, based on analyses of 1989 Federal Reserve figures, were released showing that the United States has become the most economically stratified of all industrial nations.[14] This disparity is widely expected to worsen with the initiatives of a Republican-dominated Congress, and the consequences for the homeless, as Maier (1986) suggests, are horrendous.

Belcher and Singer (1988) highlight factors operating within the U.S. economy, in particular the shortsighted decisions of government-as-welfare-state, in analyzing this disparity. At the beginning of the 1980s, unemployment was at a post-war high; accompanying this was high inflation, low production, and a stagnating economy. Businesses laid off thousands of workers, whose employer became, effectively, the welfare state. In the late 1980s the economy recovered, but, as Belcher and Singer contend, the numbers of jobless and marginally employed continued to escalate. And since, they argue, the taxes paid by large corporations could not cover the costs of welfare benefits for unemployed or homeless people, the welfare state, fearing overseas flight of corporate investment, and thus even more joblessness, centered its efforts on keeping corporate tax rates low. Belcher and Singer argue that this focus was misplaced, leading to another downward spiral of joblessness, homelessness, and, thus, increased economic stratification.

Most researchers agree that the effects of the economic crises of the deindustrtialization of the 1980s (Newman 1985) were drastically compounded for the poor by Reaganomics, and in particular the housing policies of the Reagan administration that were continued in the Bush years. Reaganomics is generally seen as a primary cause of homelessness in the United States.

Ronald Reagan's housing policy had two mutually reinforcing goals. The first was to stop all federal programs that subsidized the construction of low-income housing. Since the 1930s, the federal government had guaranteed mortgages at minimal interest rates to builders of low-cost housing. The owners of these buildings held 20-year contracts to offer apartments to eligible people at what federal and local governments determined as a fair market price. Families would pay up to 30% of their income in rent, and the balance would be paid by the government. After 20 years, the contract between government and building owner would expire, and the landlord was then free to raise rents to whatever the market would bear. Usually this meant that

23

rents at least doubled, forcing all of the low-income people in the building to move out.

But before 1980, as old housing contracts expired, new units were being built under the same program, so the situation, while not good, was not disastrous. But in the Reagan-Bush years, as old buildings went on the market no new buildings were erected to replace them. Since 1980, people who were forced out of subsidized apartments could find no new, subsidized places to go, and many of these people became homeless. By the year 2000, twenty years after the last housing contracts were signed, this program will cease to exist.

The only type of federal housing aid available under Reagan's policies was the Section Eight program, which provided rent aid in the form of coupons. These coupons, with a fixed dollar amount, could be used as partial payment on apartments whose rents were under a certain fair price. But since most of the fair price housing has disappeared, Section Eight coupons are often essentially worthless, since they cannot be used to help pay higher rents. In New York City, HUD estimates, as many as 80% of all coupons issued each month were typically returned.

A report issued by two New York-based advocacy organizations, the Association for Neighborhood and Housing Development and the Housing Justice Campaign, argues that "the City did and does have substantial power to affect how these larger forces play out in New York, who benefits from them, [and] who pays the heaviest price" (Brower 1989). But almost without exception, argues the report's author, Bonnie Brower, the city's policies have only made the situation of the poor worse, subsidizing housing for the middle classes while displacing the poor and racial minorities. For example, under the City's 1985 Ten Year Housing Plan, low income families earning less than $10,000 are eligible for just 87 units—0.3%—of the 84,000 new subsidized apartments proposed (ibid). The City's rationale is that neighborhood stability requires a mixed income population, but the outrageously small percentage of housing allocated to the most needy suggests another rationale: that neighborhood stability requires minute percentages of poor people.

Another important factor in the depletion of low-income housing stock in New York City is fire damage; in a 1985 study, the Human Resources Administration found that fires accounted for the displacement of as many as 28% of the people it surveyed. In examining this issue, class- and race-based City politics again come to the fore. Wallace (1989) notes that in 1967-68, after fire rates in ghetto areas of New York skyrocketed, 20 fire companies were opened in the affected neighborhoods. But in 1972, the city cited austerity measures to justify its decision to close or relocate 35 fire companies from poor or ghetto neighboorhoods. At the same time, city guidelines established new limited response policies in these neighborhoods. Wallace terms the predictable result a "contagious destruction" of poor and minority neighbor-

24

hoods, with more than 10,000 low-income units lost in the years between 1975-78 alone. This chilling decimation of countless neighborhoods was sealed with the equally predictable outmigration of whites from affected areas.

And given that only 87 units of the City's Ten Year Plan are targeted for the poorest city residents, many of these people are, in the words of Dwayne Pope, a former law student from the Bronx who himself was burned out of his childhood home, "burned twice—by the fire and by the city."

THE TRYANNY OF TERMINOLOGY: "DISAFFILIATION"

The reluctance of the houselessness literature to consider cultural explanations becomes understandable in light of the general rubric under which cultural factors that underlie homelessness are typically considered in certain segments of the social science literature: "disaffiliation."

Disaffilitaion is defined as social dysfunction; it is "the absence or attenuation of the affiliative bonds that link settled persons to a network of interconnected social structures.... This theory links family instability in the family of origin to undersocialization, and is hypothesized to lead to social withdrawl" (Jackson-Wilson and Borgers 1993: 363).

The disaffiliation literature (e.g., Bahr, 1970, 1973; Bachrach, 1984; Mitchell, 1987; Ropers, 1988; Rossi, 1989; and Bassuk, 1990) strives to understand why some marginally employed and tenuously housed people become homeless while others do not. It undercuts this aim, however, with a narrow methodology utilizing various acronymic instruments (e.g., SSQ, the Social Support Questionnaire, FACES III, which tests for family adaptability and cohesiveness, and F-COPE, which measures a family's ability to cope with crisis) which indicate the basic assumptions and conclusions of this approach—that family cohesion helps prevent homelessness. The kind of generalized definitions of cohesion, and of family, used in the disaffiliation literature have long been attacked for their ethnocentrism; in one of the most well-known examples, Carol Stack (in *All Our Kin*, 1974) found extensive social ties and strong kin networks among what were seen as socially dysfunctional black families.

In addition, the disaffiliation and disaffection with dominant institutions that can be found among homeless people exists among nonhomeless people as well, and can be seen as pointing to a problem with the nuclear family imperative instead of as indexical of the psychological or social dysfunctions of people who choose to leave families. Families can be strong and yet damaging to their members, and disaffiliation can be an active and thoughtful choice rather than a missed opportunity, as a brave decision to leave a pathological situation. By using family cohesion as an indicator of individual or social health, the disaffiliation literature mistakes the symptom—problems within nuclear families—for the disease, which I am arguing is the imperative of family.

A similar problem of interpretation exists in analyses of two of the other personal characteristics that are often cited as causes of homelessness—substance abuse and mental illness. These are often subsumed under the disaffiliation rubric as factors leading to the disintegration of an individual's social ties.

Discussions of substance abuse and mental illness among homeless populations are the arenas in which much of the victim-blaming of homeless people tends to occur. In 1992, for instance, *New York Times* journalist Walter Goodman alleged that the public was being duped by unwarranted, sympathetic views of homelessness. Goodman complained that the media's tendency to depict homelesss people as the deserving poor "conflict[s] with the statistics":

> The report this week that more than two-thirds of the single men and almost a third of the adults in families housed in New York City's shelters are on drugs or alcohol may startle people who are addicted to television news. More often than not, a news story or documentary on the homeless will feature a hard-working, straight-living young couple or an attractive teenager and her child who have run into a spell of bad luck.[15]

Though I think Goodman draws the wrong conclusions, he makes a good point in reference to transparent attempts by the media to generate sympathy for the homeless by depicting families or single mothers who are "just like middle-class you and me," but down on their luck. (The irony is, of course, that even if such a family were to become homeless, it would not remain so for long.) Media images of other homeless people, the people who likely will never be housed, are rarer. But is this, as Goodman suggests, because they don't deserve to be housed? These assumptions are precisely those which the houselessness literature counters best in its elucidation of the structural—as opposed to moral—determinants of poverty.

In addition, Goodman's "on drugs or alcohol" scare tactics are misleading. The study Goodman refers to defines substance abuse as "alcohol use daily or drug use monthly"—not necessarily an indication of the kind of depraved addiction his rhetoric implies. The results of the report Goodman uses, compiled by a team headed by Andrew Cuomo, are unremarkable, but Goodman's outrage at what he calls "the truth" perpetuates a damaging lie: that people are poor, or homeless, because of their bad values.

Other studies on the incidence of substance abuse within the homeless population estimate that between 30 and 40% abuse drugs and/or alcohol (e.g., HUD 1989). Wright and Weber (1987) have found that 50% of homeless men and 16% of homeless women abuse alcohol, while in a separate study Wright (1988) has found that equal numbers (13%) of homeless men and women are drug addicts.

In addition to problems of defining what constitutes abuse of or addiction to legal or illegal substances, the figures on drug and alcohol abuse alone cannot address a more pressing concern—whether drug/alcohol use is a cause or an effect of homelessness and poverty. Many researchers link the high incidence of drug use among poor and minority populations to the despair and hopelessness that characterize the lives of most urban poor today (e.g. Hopper, 1987, Marcuse, 1988, Wagner, 1994). Clearly, on a individual basis, drug use can be either a cause or an effect—or both—of homelessness. But rhetoric that translates substance abuse into a moral transgression that deserves the punishment of homelessness does not shed light on either problem, nor is it intended to.

Discussions of mental illness as a cause of homelessness less frequently end up in the same analytic dead-end. This is perhaps because one focus of the houselessness literature has been on the economics of deinstitutionalizing the hospitalized mentally ill, a trend that began in the 1970s.

E. Fuller Torrey, a former National Institute for Mental Health psychiatrist, points to what he calls a "politics of perdition" that led to the massive deinstitutionalization of mentally ill people in the early 1970s (1988). Torrey isolates 1961 as a "watershed year for psychiatric services" (1988: 97); that year saw the publication of four crucial documents: Erving Goffman's *Asylums*, *The Myth of Mental Illness* by Thomas Szasz, Gerald Caplan's *An Approach to Community Mental Health*, and the publication of the Joint Commission on Mental Illness and Health's long-awaited report. Ken Kesey's *One Flew Over the Cuckoo's Nest* followed the next year; he, along with Goffman and Szasz, promoted a vision of mental illness as largely created within oppressive "total institutions." Kesey's heroic images of Randle McMurphy and Chief Broom fighting the evil Nurse Ratched were powerful and persuasive among the left, Torrey argues, and he concludes that leftist concerns, which were inadvertently furthered by the irrational and overblown scare-tactics of McCarthyism,[16] were powerful forces in producing what he calls the "nightmare of deinstitutionalization."

27

Indictments of mental institutions, however, came from all sides; even the head of the American Psychiatric Association, Harry C. Solomon, called for their abolition in 1958 (Solomon, 1958). And in 1963 President John F. Kennedy, whose sister Rosemary was institutionalized, signed legislation calling for the creation of community mental health centers (CMHCs) to promote mental health and to treat mildly retarded and mentally ill people. This legislation provided that CMHCs be primarily funded by the states instead of the federal government, which funded state mental hospitals. This gave the federal government an opportunity to save money, which Torrey argues it took with a vengeance: by the end of Ronald Reagan's first term as president, 80% (or 433,404) of the total number of beds in state mental hospitals were taken out of use.

Torrey, thus, attributes the dramatic rise in houselessness to deinstitutionalization. Kim Hopper, an anthropologist and former president of the Coalition for the Homeless, has generally and vehemently denied Torrey's argument. Hopper argues that deinstitutionalization was largely accomplished before 1975, and that homelessness only began to accelerate in the early 1980s. While Hopper does not deny that there are mentally ill people who are homeless, he argues that this perspective is far too limited to understand, or to address, the problems of homelessness. David Snow et al. (1986) agree, arguing that it is a cultural (and comfortable) myth that mental illness can explain away the phenomenon of homelessness. Christopher Jencks (1994) stakes out a middle position, arguing that deinstitutionalization was not over by 1975, and that the phase after 1975 was so poorly managed that it led to significant numbers of former hospital residents becoming homeless.

In recent years, New York City has seen an alarming escalation of reports of homeless mentally ill and violent men stalking or attacking women, harassing passers-by, and following children. The cases that have received the most press attention have typically been in "good neighborhoods"; indeed, since the summer of 1992, much of that coverage focused on one homeless man, Larry Hogue, who continually returned to terrorize his old neighborhood of the Upper West Side every time he was released from psychiatric observation. Hogue's case led to calls for the creation of a new diagnosis by New York State psychiatrists that would provide a basis for his long-term commitment; this kind of preventive diagnosis had disappeared with deinstitutionalization.

28

The case of Larry Hogue, the uproar accompanying the January 1993 beating death of Doll Johnson, an 80-year-old woman who was killed while walking down the steps of a Brooklyn church, and other high profile incidents are leading to changes in City mental health policy. Ms. Johnson's assailant was a homeless mentally ill man who lived in a special "yellow zone" for disturbed people in a Bronx shelter; the existence of that yellow zone, though, did not mean that any extra care or special attention was given to people living within it. On January 21, 1993, the City ordered that all shelter residents be examined in order to identify and hospitalize those whose mental states were deemed dangerous.

This understandable reaction raises the specter of Kesey's Randle McMurphy: do we preventively hospitalize people who might be dangerous, or do we ignore warning signs and wait until someone is killed? Or do we, as Kim Hopper advocates, address the social and economic causes of many homeless people's mental illness—life in horrifying and inhuman conditions? This question is equally applicable to substance abuse and disaffiliation in general—do we want to, in good faith, address the underlying causes of these problems, or are we content to treat the symptoms, blame the victims, and ignore the diseases?

THE CULTURAL LOGIC OF "HOMELESSNESS"

What is missing in the houselessness literature, and poorly conceptualized or absent in the disaffiliation literature broadly defined, is an analysis of the process of remaining homeless, as opposed to becoming houseless.[17] That process, I have found, is neither transparent nor random; it is, rather, a cultural expression of deeply-entrenched beliefs about the relative worth of different genders and races of people.

Homelessness is, as Redburn and Buss (1986) argue, less an absolute condition than a series of deprivations of varying degrees. This fluidity of status is emphasized in the definition of homelessness used in the Stewart B. McKinney Homeless Assistance Act of 1987, the first comprehensive federal response to homelessness. In the provisions of the McKinney Act, a homeless person is broadly defined as someone who "lacks a fixed, regular and adequate nighttime residence," or else as someone who "has a primary night residence that is a shelter or other type of supervised, temporary living accommodation, or sleeps in a public or private place not designed for or ordinarily used as a regular sleeping accommodation for human beings."

For some people, homelessness comes relatively suddenly, with job loss and a subsequent eviction. For others, as Ellen Bassuk argues, "homelessness is often the final stage in a lifelong series of crises and missed opportunities, the culmination of a gradual disengagement from supportive relationships and institutions" (Bassuk, 1984: 43). From this perspective, the process of becoming and remaining homeless resembles Igor Kopytoff's description of slavery: slavery is "not…a fixed and unitary status, but…a process of social transformation that involves a succession of phases and changes in status, some of which merge with other statuses… that we in the West consider far removed from slavery" (1986: 65).

29

Kopytoff's description is relevant to the process of remaining homeless at a second level as well: certain kinds or statuses of homeless New Yorkers, primarily women and their children, inflected by other "statuses," such as race, are given the chance to move all the way through the shelter system to a subsidized apartment, while other statuses, particularly African-American childless men, can expect to remain homeless for years, if not for life. The status of homelessness merges with gender and racial stereotypes to produce a pattern of discrimination perpetuated by social welfare legislation, the evaluative practices of social service personnel, and the evaluative practices of the rest of us, who daily decide which homeless people deserve our money or our sympathy.

The outcome of these practices is that families stay homeless for far shorter periods than do single adults; this, I will argue below, is one consequence of the very concept of "homelessness." As Redburn and Buss contend, homeless people have less in common than might ordinarily be expected. In particular, I would argue, they don't even all share homelessness, if we define "home" as a specific network of human relationships that sometimes resides in a "house." It is houseless families who will be rehoused, while homeless, childless adults will be left to the streets.

Sophie Watson and Helen Austerberry (1986), in one of the best efforts to theorize homelessness, have argued that "a problem with the concept of homelessness is the notion of a 'home.' A 'house' is generally taken to be synonymous with a dwelling or physical structure, whereas a 'home' is not. A 'home' implies particular social relations..." (ibid: 8). These social relations are those of the nuclear family.

That we do not call unsheltered people "houseless," but "homeless," is revealing of the twin functions of the nuclear family as the normative unit of both social and spatial organization. Houses are family "homes," and housing policy is family policy. This was made abundantly clear in 1931, when the Hoover Commission Report on *Home Building and Home Ownership* dashed the dreams of communitarians for publicly-funded and broadly supported cooperative communities. The Commission chose to advocate instead that federally subsidized mortgages be given only toward single-family home ownership, and only to men of "sound character and industrious habit" (Hayden, 1981: 22). Since that report was issued, the federal government has subsidized the construction of 50 million single-family homes.

Our housing policies today, for both homeless and nonhomeless, are much the same. Despite trends of the past 25 years, which have seen the percentage of Americans living alone jump from 3 to 11%—totaling 23 million American adults in 1990, according to Census figures—housing policy is still family policy, in that the housing subsidies that exist are primarily for families. But although the dominant ideology of home—the nuclear family imperative—restricts the choices available to all Americans, the impact of that institutionalized ideology is clearest when we look at the lives of people who have few defenses against the dictates of social policy—the homeless.

Home is Where the Blood Is

> The territory of home gets into our blood, somehow, and our address comes to be as much a part of our being as anything else. (Perin, 1988: 63)

> **Home**, n. A house, apartment or other shelter that is the usual residence of a person, family or household; the place in which a person's domestic affections are centered....A person's native place or own country. (*Random House Dictionary of the English Language*, Unabridged 2nd edition, 1987.)

> The foundation of our free institutions is in our love, as a people, for our homes. The strength of our country is found, not in the declaration that

all men are free and equal, but in the quiet influence of the fireside, the
bonds which unite together the family circle. The corner stone of our
republic is the hearth stone. (Eliot, *Lectures to Young Women*, 1853: 55–56)

The above definitions and references to home begin to point to the
significance of "home" in the problem of homelessness. Anthropologist Grant
McCracken, in a recent interview in which he discussed the symbolic content
of objects within the home, items which create a feeling of "homeyness,"
argued that "knocking homeyness is like knocking motherhood".[18] In this
section I want to paraphrase McCracken and suggest that to invoke (or knock)
home is indeed to invoke (or knock) motherhood and, by extension, the
nuclear family, the normative unit of the home.

A home is delimited by walls; it is as much about exclusion as inclusion.
So, too, is the normative center of home, the nuclear family. The dominant
method for reckoning family or kinship in the United States is through the
idiom of blood, based upon the institution of the nuclear family. Kinship in
all societies is the basis of social differentiation, the most basic way in which
people define themselves in relation to the world and each other. In the
United States, within the bounded entity that is "home" exists another
bounded entity, the nuclear family; it is at home that the process of social
differentiation is continuously recreated as family members learn to reckon
kinship and difference in terms of blood ties. Thus the nuclear family, the
normative unit of social organization, is simultaneously the birthplace of social
differentiation.[19] The identities created at hearthside—race, gender, and
class—are forged in a naturalizing ideology of blood, mystifying the social
and political nature of both the process and its products. At home, the world
is split up into a series of relations and oppositions—"we" and "they"—that
appear natural.

Over the last two decades, feminist research, in particular the race/class/gen-
der linkage arguments put forth by Verena Martinez-Alier (Stolcke) and others, has excavated what was often the missing link in the earlier anthropological literature on kinship, the social production of gender and its relationship
to the production of class and race identities. This research provides a persuasive answer to David M. Schneider's famous question, "What is kinship all
about?"[20]

Martinez-Alier (1974, and as Stolcke, 1981) argues that in 19th-century
Cuba, racism was a pretext for economic exploitation. Social stratification was
accomplished and legitimated by an emphasis on the heredity of both status
and property coupled with a class-endogamous marriage pattern. She argues
that endogamy rules were necessary because of bilateral filiation, which made
control over the choice of spouse, and of female sexuality, crucial. Thus, marriage was a legal institution which regularized the inheritance of status and

31

property, and kinship was about racial identity, which, in turn, was about the creation and maintenance of gender and class hierarchies. The institution of marriage, Stolcke maintained, is an expression of practices and beliefs about blood—i.e., material and biological inheritance—that links class, race, and gender into one system of domination.

Dominguez's work (1986) in Louisiana further explores the political naturalization of racial identity. The naturalization process, Dominguez argues, depends on the hegemony of particular assumptions about "the properties of blood": "that identity is determined by blood; that blood ties, lineally and collaterally, carry social and economic rights and obligations; and that racial identity and class membership are determined by blood." Like Martinez-Alier, Dominguez argues that "property is not just a corollary of racial classification, it is also a criterion of it" (1986: 89).

Kinship, then, is all about social hierarchy.[21] It is the condition of possibility of social groups, and blood is its dominant language. Gender differences are the basis of kinship, and kinship in turn is the basis of race. In the United States today, the hierarchies of Difference based on myths about blood perpetuate a system in which particular identities—whether based on gender, race or class—are more likely to do the cooking, while other identities are more likely to determine what gets grown, by whom, and where, as well as what, if anything, gets eaten. Thus the ideology of home is the ideology of homelessness, for certain identities produced at home—"black" "men," for example—predominate among the three million people who are homeless.

SHELTER FROM THE STORM

It is ironic that homeless shelters themselves have become the kind of "total institutions" that Goffman described in *Asylums*. These shelters, as Kostas Gounis (1995) argues, dehumanize, domesticate, and debase homeless men, and are shelters only in the sense that their prime function is to shelter the general population from homelessness. Homeless shelters are the incarcerating spaces (Appadurai, 1988) of the new millenium.

The homeless people who shelters are protecting society from are men and women who transgress gender and familial norms; these transgressions, inflected by race and combined with poverty, are being criminalized. Four recent ethnographies offer painfully vivid descriptions of the increasing marginalization and rejection of particular homeless people by government agencies and mainstream society.

David Wagner, in *Checkerboard Square: Culture and Resistance in a Homeless Community* (1994), argues that homeless people are struggling to resist dominant imperatives—traditional family forms and the rules of employers and bureaucracies—and are developing alternative forms of social organization. Wagner counters traditional views of disaffiliation by presenting ethnograhic evidence indicating that while homeless people may be cut off from certain elements of mainstream society, they are not cut off from other social networks, or from each other. Many of his findings support those in this study, particularly ones relating to the nuclear family imperative and homeless people's resistance to it. Wagner conceptualizes this resistance as leading to the development of subcultures, as many other researchers have also viewed resistance in other contexts (see, e.g., Snow and Anderson, 1993; Willis, 1977; MacLeod, 1987).[22]

Wagner argues that homeless people are harshly penalized for avoiding traditional family forms. The people of "Checkerboard Square," located within a largely white northeastern city, "express a cynical and critical view of the family" (1994: 45), and many have suffered emotional and physical abuse. Wagner argues that homeless advocates need to have the courage to counter prevailing social fictions, such as "families are loving," instead of trying to force homeless people into societal molds.

Other recent work on the relationship of homelessness and race by Hopper (1995) and Allan Feldman (1995) augment Wagner's study and support my contention here—that it is not only family status that is being penalized, but also, and crucially, race.

Feldman (1995) argues that a unilateral and colonialesque abandonment of the public sector is now taking place in New York and across the country. He contends that educational and service institutions are being dismembered while funds are being redirected to the construction of prisons. Feldman conceptualizes the position of homelessness as "advanced marginality," and he argues persuasively that the withdrawal of services from the public sphere is nothing less than brutal, structural violence.[23] Hopper (1995) echoes Feldman's arguments, emphasizing that the overwhelming majority of victims of this violence are black men. At a recent Society for Cultural Anthropology meeting, in May 1995, Feldman argued, "We can't let this happen again, not without a fight. We, as anthropologists, have got to do something this time."

Anthropologists have sometimes been criticized for what Orin Starn has called "missing the revolution"; this was the case, for instance, in Nancy Scheper-Hughes's recent critique of Clifford Geertz.[24] Scheper-Hughes argued that Geertz's work never took into account or anticipated the purges and massacres that occurred before and after his fieldwork in Java and Morocco. Brackette Williams organized the 1995 SCA meetings at which Hopper, Feldman, Gounis and I spoke on "States of Violence and The Violence of Status"; the explicit aim was to push contemporary anthropologists to the forefront of new battlefields instead of abandoning them for more stable field sites. Williams, there and in a 1995 article in *Current Anthropology*, argued that we as anthropologists must do what she calls "homework," that we must take a self-consciously moral and political stand on the world around us.

33

This study is my own attempt at doing my "homework," for it is an attempt to further our understanding of the persistence of homelessness in an effort to begin to find permanent solutions to it. Homelessness persists in New York in large part because the people who remain homeless challenge dominant beliefs about family, gender, and race. And while the solution to homelessness must ultimately be economic, that economic cost must be seen by the majority to have a benefit. That benefit—the reaffirmation of all people's common humanity—can only be seen once we challenge the mystifying and divisive discourses of gender and race difference.

BEYOND THE PANOPTICON

The Nuclear Family, Men, and Social Control

We are living at an important and fruitful moment now, for it is clear to men that the images of adult manhood given by the popular culture are worn out; a man can no longer depend on them. By the time a man is thirty-five he knows that the images of the right man, the true man which he received in high school do not work in life. Such a man is open to new visions of what a man is or could be. (Bly 1990:ix)

chapter 3

WITH THESE words, Marc Greenberg, the director of the Interfaith Assembly on Homelessness and Housing, opened a monthly reunion of homeless graduates of a self-help/outreach program. The meeting took place in the early fall of 1990 in the cavernous basement of the Cathedral of Saint John the Divine in Harlem. The men present had all recently graduated from the Assembly's Education Outreach Program, and they continued to meet each month to share a meal and to map out their next steps. I was there because Marc had asked for my help in making a fundraising film featuring some of the graduates. Before the meal, each person spoke about why s/he was there, what their immediate goals were, and what they were feeling. Marc and I were included in the circle, and I at least spoke with my heart in my throat—I had many of the same problems with frustration and motivation as these men reported, but mine were largely confined to the rarified realm of dissertation research rather than to physical and spiritual survival. The last person to speak was a quiet and reflective man named Pat Flanagan,[1] who talked about a letter he had just received from his daughter, a senior at the University of Southern California. He said, "I think she understands now why I left my family.... She seems like she understands that homelessness was something I had to do for myself."

Pat went on to describe homelessness as space within which he could work on and discover himself and his feelings. He decided to leave his family and become homeless because he wanted "time out" from the responsibilities that he had always accepted but that left him feeling like "I was the only one who didn't get a chance to grow, to explore." In order to fulfill himself as a human being, Pat felt that he had to free himself from his role as breadwinner.

The theme of restrictive gender roles as somehow implicated in precipitating homelessness, and of homelessness as a negation of the expectations and perquisites of gender, is not unique to Pat. I have found that across races and classes of origin, difficulties living within the limits of gender in nuclear family structures were commonly reported by homeless women and men. Many homeless men and women are refusing to continue to perform normative ideals of gender, with catastrophic results. This refusal is not unique to homeless people, but the results are: many others of us can retool our gender performances and even lose our families without losing our homes.

In this chapter, I will explore the ways in which homeless men discuss their experiences and point to gender socialization and expectations as problems that are implicated in their homelessness. In the period from 1990–93, I formally interviewed over 200 homeless men. I met the men in various ways: randomly in parks or on street corners; through my association with the Interfaith Assembly, Homeward Bound, or other organizations with which I was associated; at the Saint Francis Xavier welfare rights clinic, held each Sunday during the church's soup kitchen hours; at demonstrations in Tompkins Square Park; and at a variety of other locations. Of the 202 men I interviewed, 31 men described their homelessness as the result of rejecting breadwinner imperatives; 9 men left abusive families; 14 men felt that they did not fit masculine ideals and felt somehow that this basic, general failure eventually led to their homelessness, and 42 men, all black and hispanic, felt that poverty and race had prevented them from ever having a chance at success, at being "real" men.[2]

Male homelessness is, as I have come to see it, a space for society's rejects, the transgressors of social identity—men who refuse to be breadwinners, non-"masculine" men, young men who have been the victims of abuse within nuclear families, and men who are tainted twice, because of poverty and race, and who will most likely never get the chance to be "men." Homelessness indexes the failures of these men against the ideals of Traditional Manhood.

This is not the case, as I will argue in the next chapter, for most homeless women. Homeless women, unable to provide for themselves and their families and dependent on the paternal welfare state, are not seen as failures as women; they are, rather, the incarnation of "Woman," and they will be housed because they "belong" at home.

But when men become homeless, for whatever the reason, they experience an excruciating gender crisis; not only are they not successful men, they are not even men. As Rupert, a homeless man from Jamaica I met at the Saint Francis Xavier welfare rights clinic, explained as he was waiting to speak to an attorney, "I gotta be a man and I don't know how to do it. I need a job, a place, clothes, a woman. Shit, I can't get to first base. I'm not even a man anymore. I'm just another poor beggar on the streets."

For many of these men, who are lost, frightened, hungry and full of self-hate, the words of Robert Bly resonate with their pain as no other analysis can.

THE TWILIGHT ZONE: HOMELESSNESS AND MASCULINITY

The men present at the Assembly meeting that fall night were moved and inspired by Marc's opening reading, and many asked to look at the source, Robert Bly's *Iron John*, throughout the evening. Later that week I wrote Bly's publisher, Addison Wesley, to request that copies of *Iron John* be donated to the Assembly so that interested men could read it at their own pace. The publishers, and Bly, graciously agreed.

During the winter and spring of 1990-91 I talked with a number of men, in and out of the Assembly, who had read or were still reading *Iron John*. Each of them felt that he was on a road to recovery—from substance abuse, from leaving family members behind, from the death of parents and loved ones, and from being shuttled among myriad foster homes, among other traumas—and each felt that reading Bly's book was helping him heal.

I knew all of these men before they had read Bly, and each had already tried to come to terms with the past: How did he become homeless? What kinds of issues were involved? What mistakes were made, lessons learned? These men saw their struggles as being not so much against homelessness as against confusion, low self-esteem, and an absence of a vision for the future. For each of these men, the questions facing them seemed to have lonely, individual answers until Robert Bly articulated them in terms of the broader struggles facing all contemporary American men. Of particular relevance to them was Bly's periodization of the changing male psyche:

> We talk a great deal about "the American man," as if there
> were some constant quality that remained stable over decades, or
> even within a single decade....
> Even in our own era the agreed-upon model has changed
> dramatically. During the fifties, for example, an American character

appeared with some consistency that became a model of manhood adopted by many men: the Fifties male.

He got to work early, labored responsibly, supported his wife and children, and admired discipline. Reagan is a sort of mummified version of this dogged type. This sort of man didn't see women's souls well, but he appreciated their bodies.... Many of his qualities were strong and positive, but underneath the charm and bluff there was, and there remains, much isolation, deprivation and passivity. Unless he has an enemy, he isn't sure that he is alive....

During the sixties, another sort of man appeared. The waste and violence of the Vietnam war made men question whether they knew what an adult male really was. If manhood meant Vietnam, did they want any part of it? Meanwhile, the feminist movement encouraged men to actually look at women, forcing them to become conscious of concerns and sufferings that the Fifties male labored to avoid. As men began to examine women's history and women's sensibility, some men began to notice what was called their feminine side and pay attention to it. This process continues to this day, and I would say that most contemporary men are involved in it in some way....

In the seventies I began to see all over the country a phenomenon that we might call the "soft male." Sometimes even today when I look out at an audience, perhaps half the young males are what I'd call soft. They're lovely, valuable people—I like them—they're not interested in harming the earth or starting wars....

But many of these men are not happy. You quickly notice the lack of energy in them. They are lifepreserving but not exactly life-giving. Ironically, you often see these men with strong women who radiate positive energy....

The strong or life-giving women who graduated from the sixties, so to speak, or who have inherited an older spirit, played an important part in producing this life-preserving, but not life-giving, man. (Bly, 1990:1-2)

Bly's analysis resonated with these men. They had vaguely sensed that the problems they had were bigger than homelessness and had something to do with being men, and Bly gave their situations, and their pain, a name and an etiology. "It helps with the self-hate, to hear him," Pat said. "I made decisions with my life not always knowing why. It calms me down, to hear that other people feel the same way."

Pat found Bly's description of the contemporary "soft male" dilemma "exactly right. We're supposed to be Fifties men. There are no other heroes; we can't live up." All of the men agreed with Pat in feeling that the early pages of the book described their situation. Fred said, "I'm a '90s man born in '40 and raised in the '50s and '60s. It's a disaster."

Pat said that he felt society was ambivalent about masculinity. He described growing up as a time when his parents tried to squash his boyish exuberance and "what they saw as aggression," squashing him in the process, but because he was a boy, "they never thought to teach me to understand, express and manage my own feelings." He explained:

> When you're a kid and you hang around and respond to all the stimulus in the world, you're a problem, a nuisance. You've got to behave, be orderly. A lot of people took it upon themselves to get me to behave, to take care of what they saw as aggression. And it worked—I was depressed. My personality had been successfully depressed. I sat properly, I behaved correctly, and I was depressed. There was a morbid sense that I was a bad boy, and had to behave well.
>
> Adolescence combined with alcohol took care of growing pains, but I really didn't grow much because of the alcohol. Girls, sex, I bypassed that. I modulated my feelings with alcohol and saw myself as far more successful when I was drunk than the scared, anxious kid I was.
>
> That [drinking] went on pretty much through college. Shortly afterwards I found myself married; shortly afterwards I found myself with four kids. And I had a job, working with overhead projectors teaching people to communicate. I was nervous, I had no confidence. I ran away from what would have been a successful career to be in a full-time alcoholic stupor. I rejected my family, but I would watch my kids, saying "I can't be all bad, I got good kids."

Pat left his wife and children, feeling overwhelmed by his increasing sense of isolation and despair and frightened about how "manic" and "full of seething hate" he would get. He knew he needed help, and he didn't know how to get it. He left home and became homeless, a move that fueled his self-hate even as it gave him the opportunity to begin to "work on myself, discover what I'm about…. I'm homeless, I've got time to think and figure out without the demands of other people, my family, crowding me out."

Pat described becoming homeless as his only chance to focus on his own, rather than his wife's and kids', problems—"homelessness was something I had to do for myself." He felt that being the breadwinner meant that everyone else came first, that he existed to help fulfill his family members' lives, but that no one helped him fulfill his own.

Kenneth, another of the men who had read Bly, felt that the dilemma of the "soft" male was his:

> I'm not gay, but I'm gentle. Everyone, women and men, always says I have doe eyes. But he's [Bly] right—I have no life force. I'm quiet, I like to read, I write occasionally. But I'm not motivated for success; I was always told that from when I was young. I just want peace, and to be happy. And that's not enough.
>
> When I was a kid I was messed up, I didn't fit anywhere. I didn't feel like playing ball, but it's not that I liked dolls, nothin' like that, I just stayed to myself, quiet. In school and on my block, I was the loner, the kid they threw shit at. To this day I feel the same.

Ulysses Peter Malvan was present when Kenneth was speaking, and he took exception, he said, to how happiness was usually defined. Peter continued,

> And what is happiness? Money? Not for me. But this isn't happiness either. I have good values, I care for people, I nursed my mother until she died, I stayed with them, I cooked and cleaned for them. When they died, my mother and then my father, they were my life, I became so depressed. Was that the wrong thing to do? I just couldn't concentrate anymore, I had made caring for them my whole life. Sometimes being a human being and making money don't go together.

Like Kenneth, Peter found that some human attributes-gentleness, kindness, caring for others—were not valued in men unless they were accompanied by more typically masculine traits—independence, aggression, ambition. He explains his life in Corona, Queens, this way:

> When I was fourteen-years-old I started to have to assume responsibility because my father, who was a mortician as well as a printer, he had a stroke and he became [in]continent and he had trouble walking and he couldn't feed himself and he had trouble speaking. My mother had cardiopulmonary disease and in 1978 she had a heart attack.
>
> My sister decided to leave home not to be, like, depressed, and went into the United States Army. I stayed home, and I

became the support for my family, the taxes had to be paid. What I did was, my neighborhood, it was a cross between a black ghetto and a democratic black neighborhood. In New York we have state Lotto. Its precursor was the illegal numbers racket. I was employed in that, transferring numbers from one location to another and transferring money from one place to another.

In 1984 my mother, she died, and since I had partly taken care of her and had responsibility for taking care of my father, I got extremely depressed. My sister came home and decided that we had to put my father in a nursing home. At the time I had done two years at Queensborough Community College. Unfortunately, I didn't know how to do anything. And since I didn't know anything but taking care of my parents and illegal gambling I took a job as a home attendant after my mother died. As I said, when my sister came home she wanted to put my father in a nursing home and since she was a nurse I agreed. And we did, but I wasn't gonna lose my father, 'cause I had already lost my mother. And I spent three days a week visiting my father because my parents had become my life.

Over a three-year period I went from a jolly 200-pound man to an 83-pound walking skeleton. I lost my ability to function on my job in illegal gambling because I couldn't even count the grocery list, much less figure up a list of three digit numbers, there might be a set of 200. So I was taken out of one of my livelihoods, and when I lost so much strength both of my livelihoods were gone.

My father died in 1988. At that point my sister had married a gentleman who happened to be a cocaine user, and he graduated to crack. They sold my house to get him out of debt, my sister agreed to sell my house out from under me basically. I was an 83-pound man and I wasn't eating, and she did what she had to do and she moved to Texas.

In June of 1988, my father died on May 16th, I was evicted from my home that I lived in for thirty years by the police. I took all the documents pertaining to taxes and bills (my mother kept all the documents, she was a very good record keeper) to my grandmother's house on Long Island. After a couple of weeks I basically had to leave. My sister had told my grandmother that I had money when all I had was a hundred dollars, and my grandmother and the neighbors suspected me of being a crack addict because I was a skeleton.

41

I went into the subways. My whole dream was, actually I was irrational, but my whole dream was that I would be able to return to my home, and go into my backyard, lie down in the snow wanting to die. I had the idea that I would be with my mother, my father and my dog. It would be sort of a heaven.

But then I began to see other people, um, there were men and women on the subways who were incontinent like my father, there were people who were constantly harassed by the police whose job it was to make sure they weren't present in the mornings for rush hour, because people had to get to work and people don't look at you when you're dirty and smelly and you're laying where they want to sit. They don't look at you as an unfortunate person, they look at you as an impediment to their functioning. And the police were basically ordered to get people out of the way for rush hour.

I went to the 83rd Street shelter, where ignorance and rumor ruled. I did not want to stay there. I was told no funding for twenty-five days [when he applied for welfare]. I felt that twenty-five days was a test—you're worthless unless you can survive these twenty-five days. I decided I want to live through this. I saw other people living in the streets going through hell— handicapped, incontinent, victims of crimes. I decided I had no time to die, I was going to live and change things.

So I went from the subways to Battery Park, at the southern tip of Manhattan. I live in Castle Clinton National Monument, it's a round building that has about 26 gun ports like very deep windows. The encampment is my community, my family, now.

Peter relates to Bly because he feels that he made good choices for his own moral sense, but bad ones in the eyes of society: "I was good to my parents, I put them above myself, they were my life. Men aren't supposed to do that, there's no role models for that." Peter continues to care-take now, as a homeless man: he volunteers full-time at information tables at soup kitchens across Manhattan, helping other homeless people find their way to food, shelter, and clothing donations. Mayor David Dinkins honored Peter's work by presenting him with a Certificate of Recognition in 1991 (see figure 3.1). After his initial application for welfare, when he was told he had to wait twenty-five days for help, Peter changed his mind, deciding that he did not want whatever it was welfare offered. For the three years since then, Peter has refused to reapply.

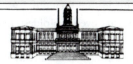

CITY OF NEW YORK

Know ye by these presents that I

David N. Dinkins

Mayor of the City of New York

do hereby present this

CERTIFICATE OF RECOGNITION

to
Ulysses Peter Malvan

for his devotion to helping the homeless learn where to find help.

*In witness whereof, I have hereunto
set my hand and caused the Seal of the
City of New York to be affixed this*
Twenty-Second day of
October 1991

43

Figure 3.1

Aldo's story is almost the opposite of Peter's; he was not raised to care-take but to be the man of the house.

> I was raised to be strong, "the little man." They called me Junior until I was 18 and I said "no more! I'm me!" My sisters were told to mind me, I made sure they did, I was like a parent, an authority figure, I wasn't even the oldest, my sister Anna was. But I was in charge. I got extra power but a lot of work because I was the man, mama always said if daddy dies I would be the man of the house. When I was young it made me feel good. Now it's like, it was a trap.
>
> I remember watching my mother and even Anna take care of my little sister, holding her when she cried, going crazy if she even scraped her arm or leg outside. I cried once, one time that I remember, and my father told me I'd never make it on the streets. He told me never to cry again. I didn't, no matter how much things hurt, until I was homeless. Then there was nobody watching me anymore.

Aldo was describing, and reacting against, a primary function of nuclear families—the creation and vigilant maintenance of gender. In his periodization, Bly points to the isolation and deprivation of Fifties men, but he misses those same feelings in men who don't fit that ideal. Perhaps this is because Bly, and the men's movement more generally, are white, middle-class phenomena; undoubtedly a different constellation of gender attributes is predominant there, perhaps a broader, more inclusive one. But for many other men, of other races and of lower classes, gender noncompliance is more threatening, for there are fewer safety nets. Some of those safety nets are material, and class-related, but others are psychological, internalized aspects of cultural values. For Pat, a middle-aged white man, homelessness was inevitable because he was so wracked with guilt and self-hate because of his decision to leave his family. Unlike Peter, Aldo and most homeless men, in class terms Pat could have avoided homelessness, but he felt his wish to take "time out" from breadwinning was so incompatible with everything he was taught that he flung himself into what seemed the only appropriate space—the no-man's land of homelessness. Aldo and Peter—poor and gentle black men—were, on the other hand, flung into that space, in part because their failures as Ideal Men left them no place to go.

GREAT EXPECTATIONS

Early in November 1990, Pat, Marc Greenberg and I went with a group of homeless men and a few other friends to a production of The Living Theater's *Body of God*, an interactionist play about homelessness performed by homeless people in a rundown but well-known theater on Manhattan's Lower East Side. Among the goals of the performers were to challenge, to move, and to equalize, and many of their techniques were effective. Upon entering each person in the audience was given a cardboard box and a shopping bag; the boxes became our seats and we were asked to put our belongings in the bags. The Burberry trenchcoats, leather jackets, navy surplus pea jackets, and overcoats of space-age plastic quickly vanished, and for the remainder of the evening it was hoped that people would respond to each other's words instead of their status markers.

One of the people we met that evening was Gary, a former vice-president of Banker's Trust with a master's degree in psychology. Gary was a member of the cast, not the audience. The first words he used to introduce himself eerily echoed Pat's: "All my life I've done what other people wanted me to do—my parents, my teachers, my boss, my wife, my kids. Now that I'm homeless I'm doing what I want to do."

After the play ended, the audience and cast broke into small group discussions. Some of my companions joined Gary's group, while others joined whichever cast member was closest to them. When the evening was over, all of us, cast and audience alike, were reluctant to leave. We had just experienced an anachronism, a 1960s-style community interaction amidst the isolation of the '90s, and none of us wanted such an abrupt ending. On the way home we talked about the life stories of all of the cast members, but discussion kept returning to Gary.

Marc and I talked about the play in the next meeting at the Cathedral. The eight men present listened, laughed, and sympathized as we related each person's story. When Marc was finished, Jose, one of the younger men, said "Man, Gary's right. Love lasts only as long as the paycheck."

I asked Jose what he meant, since that wasn't what I had heard Gary say at all. Jose told me about what happened after he lost his once-secure job, how he began to lose arguments with his wife, how she no longer seemed to respect or care about him. He finally left her, not, as in Pat's and Gary's cases, because he felt straitjacketed by his role as breadwinner, but because when he lost that role he seemed to lose his family, too. "It sucks, man, they don't love you, they love what you do for them."

Frank, who had also read Bly, agreed. "We are weak, we have let people tell us what to do, it's not okay for one person to support five other people. We work like fucking dogs but we should've stood up and said 'hey, this is not right.'"

Frank's argument is a twist on Bly's; Frank sees the weakness as beginning with 50s males' acceptance of gender roles, while Bly locates the weaknesses of 60s and 70s men in their search for alternatives to it.

The anger that these men feel is often vague and targetless, or directed scatter-shot at particular people, at themselves, or at society. When I spoke with

45

Luis, who worked as a doorman and a janitor for twenty years, he explained that he saw "no way out, like if I wanted a break. I couldn't ask my wife or the kids to go make money." He explained,

> You feel like an orange, squeezed tighter and tighter until you explode....The demands came from everywhere, my family, my job. I started snorting coke first, it made me too crazy, intense.... I started drinking after work, then at lunch, then all night watching TV. And after awhile I didn't have what it took to go into work. I completely fucked up my life. I let everyone down; my wife went to live with her aunt in Staten Island.

When I asked him if he felt that anyone had let him down, he replied,

> No, not really. Not my wife, not her, I don't know. But something, like life let me down, you know? This can't be it, all it is.

Scott, too, felt that breadwinning was an unfair burden, one that he felt his wife was (unfairly) unwilling to share. They lived most of their married life on eastern Long Island, from where he would commute over an hour each way to Manhattan:

46

> Every day, up at 5, out by 5:30, get onto the railroad and hit the city by 7:15, get coffee, donuts, at work by 8. I call my wife at noon, she's stretching, yawning, just getting going. What am I, a jerk? I kept at her to get a job, anything, she said no, she has no skills, I said answer the phones, do filing for Chrissakes. It wasn't the money, um, we could use it though, it was just to even things up.
> But I was wrong, I know that now. She left, I stopped the rat race, did nothing all day. The money ran out, no phone first, then no electric. The house was auctioned, by the bank. Now look at me, I still can't believe it.

Scott was living in a drop-in clinic when I met him, sleeping by lying across two chairs, because he found the shelters too dangerous.

Like Scott, Luis, Frank, Gary and Pat, Carl too, felt that breadwinning ideology had uneven motivating force:

> I was married twelve years. I have three kids, the oldest is 10. I don't know why I did it, what was wrong with me. But you

come home and look at the kids and say it's all worth it, these are beautiful kids, and then you forget it, I don't know, at work or with your friends, it don't make sense, live your life for the kids, but it does, you know? Now what am I living it for? Booze and sleep, and peace, that's it, the story. I moved in with my mother, my wife and kids they still live in the apartment, but how long can a grown man live with his mother?

Carl sometimes considers going back home, and he misses his family terribly. But, he says, "I don't think I belong anymore."

All of these men feel that gender has ill-served them, made failures of them simply because they wouldn't or couldn't make themselves over in the image of the Fifties man. In addition, they articulate the pain of discovering that the nuclear family is an economic as well as affiliative unit, and they feel that they no longer belong there as people, as individuals, as loved ones, if they are not willing to be there as "men," as breadwinners (see Bellah, 1985 for another discussion of this phenomenon among some of his informants). In their rejection of breadwinner roles, they feel that they have also somehow lost the very stuff of maleness.[3]

In my work among these men I found the opposite of a phenomenon Claudia Strauss (1992) reported in her study of working men in Rhode Island. Strauss argued that for the men in her study, breadwinner models were like Geertz's "native point of view," implicit rules for behavior that men had no choice but to follow. The men in Strauss's study tended not to explicitly articulate the breadwinner model, and she explained this by arguing that this model was, quoting Bourdieu, a "discourse of familiarity, [which] leaves unsaid all that goes without saying" (Bourdieu, 1977 in Strauss, 1992: 218). In contrast, the men we see here are often explicitly articulating and contesting that norm, and the result is personal disaster.

It is in this space, where old models have worn out and new models have yet to be internalized, that Bly speaks to these and other homeless men, formulating and articulating their confusion and pain as powerfully as feminism did for women three decades ago.

Most feminists are at least ambivalent about the men's movement, and part of that can be attributed to analyses like Bly's that blame men's problems on women, particularly mothers. But the ambivalence predates Bly. In 1983, Barbara Ehrenreich's *The Hearts of Men* charted the history of erosion of the motivational force of traditional men's roles, particularly that of breadwinner. She argued that men were fleeing breadwinner status for decades before feminism, and that "the male revolt," while rooted in a prefeminist "narcissistic consumer culture," can also be seen as compatible with a feminist "liberal humanism" that sees all gender roles as restrictive and disfiguring (1983: 170).

47

While Ehrenreich's take on men's dissatisfaction with their prescribed roles within nuclear families is generally much more sympathetic than most other feminists, she nonetheless complains, both here and in *Fear of Falling* (1990), that men's flights from commitment began long before feminism, and that feminism conveniently "offered a socially conscious rationale for this some-what churlish attitude" (1990: 218). But why should their flights seem churl-ish? Women's dissatisfaction with their roles certainly predates the interpretive spin of feminist liberation ideology, and feminists deplore the limits gender imperatives have placed on women. Doesn't gender also restrict men?

I make this point here because it is crucial; the discourse on men is gener-ally full of mistrust and ambivalence, and this, combined with what I see as the dangerous analyses of what Katha Pollitt calls "difference feminism," leads to the situation I will describe in Chapter Five, a convergence of ideologies and practices that leaves homeless men out on the streets while housing women and reinscribing women's traditional "place."

On the other hand, one wing of the men's movement that Bly's work helped coalesce is indeed anti-feminist—witness the specter of strong women as castrating mothers in Bly's own analysis above.[4] In this book, I am arguing that dominant ideologies about gender at best limit the options, and the per-sonalities, of all women and men, and, at worst—when failures to meet gen-der ideals are seen as indexical of social worth, those definitions can actively undermine individuals' chances for survival.

48

GENDER FAILURE, RACE SUCCESS?

The men who gain most from dominant gender ideology occupy particular positionalities—white men and middle- and upper-class men. For these men, prevalent conceptions of masculine strength buttress their claims to legitimate authority and privilege. This is not the case, however, with the men at the bot-tom—primarily black men, poor men, and homeless men. Homeless men occupy very different social positions than most men in the men's movement. They do not gain from traditional perceptions of male strength; they suffer from them. To fail at what they see as their most basic role, supporting them-selves and their families, is to fail at manhood. Homeless men often feel this way about themselves, and so does society at large.

The problems with the expectations that surround manhood are perhaps most apparent to men who have been prevented because of racism and pover-ty from ever fulfilling them. Homeless men who are black shared a relatively unique and extremely bleak perspective; most reported that neither individual success nor breadwinning were things they ever felt they could achieve. For many of these men, homelessness was less a rupture than part of a process of diminishing possibility and hope that had begun decades earlier, often in their early youth.

One of these men was Darryl, who lived in the encampment at Tompkins Square Park before it was dismantled by police in the spring of 1991. He grew up in the projects of the so-called Alphabet Jungle of the Lower East Side of Manhattan, alternately living with his drug-addict parents, relatives, and family friends until he moved into an apartment in Brooklyn with his girlfriend and their daughter. His girlfriend was an AFDC recipient; Darryl did not work, and never had.

> I felt so bad, before, I hated what I was. I never spent time at home, I was always druggin'. I been that way since I can remember, can't keep still. But I feel worse now, this is worse. At least before I was somethin', you know?

Dewon grew up in a south Bronx neighborhood characterized, like many poor neighborhoods these days, by both physical and social devastation: drugs are everywhere, people are afraid to sit by lighted windows at night, much less go outside. Dewon was raised by his grandmother; his mother was in and out of jail for drug-related crimes, and he never knew his father. I met him through Part of the Solution (POTS), a Bronx-based homeless and squatter advocacy organization. He talked about himself and his life one afternoon over a Cuban-Chinese meal.

49

> I started staying out all night, going on missions, when I was about 10 or 11. We'd hang out, party a little, ride in cars, nothin' much. There was nothin Nana could do. Everyone was like that, not just me....
>
> I don't think I ever knew anyone with a job back then. Maybe some people did, I ain't sayin they didn't, but I never thought about it.
>
> *How about school?*
>
> I been to school, sometimes, but then I just stopped. What's the point? You were playing a waiting game, sittin' there, waiting to get out. I didn't know no good students, I never thought about it, take it seriously. No one I knew graduated high school—no way, man! Well, maybe some of the girls, but that's different, what else they got to do?...
>
> It was no big thing, becoming homeless. My Nana died, how it happened. For a little while I stayed in the apartment, then they turned me out and I stayed here and there, but it was a hassle, nobody wants you on their couch for too long, you dig? I didn't expect to end up like this, but I didn't expect nothin' else

either. It's not like I thought I'd be [New York City Mayor David] Dinkins or nothin'.

Did you ever think about getting married, having kids?
Yeah I did, I thought I would, one of my ladies, sometime.

Did you feel like you'd have to get a job, to do that?
Well maybe so, I didn't think I wouldn't, let's say, but you don't need a job to have kids, you know, you get foodstamps, you get yourself hired by some of the homies, something safer maybe, see I didn't have the balls they did, that stuff was not for me, people getting killed like every night. People I knew, grew up with.

OK, how about this—did you ever think you'd be a success?
Sister, you be smokin too much reefer at that college of yours! A success? As what? The best I coulda been is a successful dope-dealin black man, living in the neighborhood, having a family, not getting dead too young.

The life Dewon describes became depressingly familiar to me; I heard variations of it almost daily. The available routes to "success," to being a man, were few; the most obvious ones, in the drug trade, were dangerous ones; you had to "have balls" to do them. Rejection of that lifestyle as too dangerous seemed to entail enormous consequences for men living in the ghettoized, routinized, generation-spanning poverty that characterizes many poor black and hispanic neighborhoods—you weren't a success, you weren't a man, and if the entitlement-receiving member of your family died or left you were homeless, in the twilight zone of gender and class.

This is especially poignant in the story that Red relates:

OK so now I'm here, figuring if I didn't make it at home, how I'm gonna make it out here? My brothers took me here, from Newark, beat the shit outta me, see you can still see where they cracked my head, they said don't come back till you're a fucking man. I'm like, I don't bring any money to the family, I got fired from my job last year, and I don't want to do what they do, it's dangerous shit. I try to stay out of their way, but it didn't work out. I feel safer here, if this shelter is halfway decent, I need to think. I heard it's dangerous, if you ain't prepared, you gotta sleep with your shoes and your coat under your head. What kind of a man can you be from here?

The dilemma that Red, Dewon, and Darryl articulate concerns the conflation of manhood, masculinity, with success. "Men" aren't afraid; "men" aren't poor; "men" aren't failures. In a racist society, success and blackness are already at odds. But because success is often defined financially, with millionaire athletes like Michael Jordan at the top of the heap, upper- and middle-class black men might be able to flatten, or at least mitigate, the contradiction. But men in lower classes, particularly minority men, are less and less able to carve out even small niches of success. While some middle class men, like Pat, are facing the contradictions between Me-Decade ideologies of individualism and gender ideology based on the nuclear family imperative, lower-class men, particularly those of color, face the opposite problem: it is increasingly difficult, if not impossible, for poor working men to successfully fulfill breadwinner roles even if they wanted to. Theoretically, these are opposite sides of the same ideological coin, in which the only way to be a man in this society is to take on the mantle of *pater familias*.

An interview with Eduardo, a 30-year-old man from Jersey City who had been homeless for four years, raised some of the specific entailments of his failure to be a "man." Towards the middle of our conversation, I realized that his initially mild flirtatiousness was becoming problematic, and I had to stop and call him on it.

> I didn't mean nothin', to make you uncomfortable. It's just …
> it's been a long time, is all, since I been with a woman. A
> homeless man is nobody's man.

51

> *Can I ask you, how long has it been, since you became homeless?*
> Naw, not that long, but even before, my woman kicked me out,
> she said she was makin' all the money and I was just spending it,
> even with her it was no good. Being poor isn't exactly what
> they want, you know, in a man.

Gender ideology can be vicious, and viciously circular, to men who fail to live up to it. Despite the fact that many of these men stand little chance of becoming or remaining "men," they are blamed—and blame themselves—for their plight because, after all, they are men:

> I feel bad, man, 'cause I'm a man, I'm supposed to be able to
> take care of myself. Instead I'm sitting here waitin' for you
> people to help us.

> When we got evicted my wife left with the kids. She's with her
> mother in Brooklyn…. I don't blame her, I'm not the man she
> married anymore.

To be a man you need a good job, a family to take care of. You need to be takin' care of people, not asking for help.

What a sorry state for a man to be in, I tell you, lady. I ain't no kinda man no more.

The circularity does not stop here. In my conversations with many men, it became clear that there remained one route open for establishing masculinity—fathering a child. Thus, while the economy makes success practically impossible, threatening men's perceptions of themselves as men, fatherhood is one gender role still open to them, one last way to secure a toehold on masculinity. But because these children are fathered by men who can't even support themselves, and because they are often unwanted except as tokens of masculinity, or else as routes to an AFDC check, many of these children will become the next generation of homeless women and men.

Enrico, a 19-year old man living at Homeward Bound, felt that he was one of these unwanted kids. He said, "I don't know why she [his mother] had me, man. She never even wanted me around. Maybe it was the welfare."

I met Enrico on Valentine's Day in 1991, when I joined a game of black-jack with a number of homeless men. When Hal, a gay man who often affected a high-pitched voice to make his friends laugh, was dealt the Queen of Hearts, he squealed and said with a flourish, "And who but me deserves the queen?" A few hands later, when Enrico was dealt the Queen of Clubs, he responded, "Ha. The Queen of Clubs. My mother." Hal looked at him and said, "Really?" and Enrico replied, "Yeah, man, like you wouldn't believe." He chuckled a bit and the game went on.

Afterwards I stayed around to talk to Enrico for a few minutes, to ask him to lunch the next day. He accepted, although he said he didn't want to talk much. "I feel so bad about it, man. It sticks with me." I asked him what he felt bad about, being homeless or being abused. "It's the same thing, man." He later told me a little about his childhood.

Yeah, well, from when I was little I would be sent to the store to buy milk, cigarettes, like that, and sometimes when I would come back the door would be locked and nobody'd answer. I could hear her [his mother] in there with someone, a guy, and I'd sit outside on the stairs. Hours man, overnight sometimes. And I'd be so scared out there, and I couldn't do my homework, and people be coming up and down all night from a crack house on the top floor.

A couple of times I was robbed of the money, and sometimes I'd buy candy and not have enough, and when I came home I'd really get it, with the belt, the chair, pots, whatever.

> To this day I hate going into those little stores. They just
> remind me, it makes me hate myself, that that happened.

Enrico felt that being abused as a child ruined his life chances—as he said
above, in response to my question about what he felt so bad about, being
homeless or being abused, he replied that it was "the same thing."
Tino, a 20-year old man living at Homeward Bound, agreed:

> I've always been homeless in my mind. I've been in eight foster
> homes since I was ten. You make one wrong move and the next
> morning your bags are packed and in the hall. My parents, my
> father was in jail, my mother was never home, we got taken away.
> I been beaten so many times, I finally got it all beaten out of me.

Being homeless for these young men seemed to be related to their experiences as children, feeling unwanted and abused by their families, "homeless"
while still at home. And yet legislation designed to protect children does so by
protecting families, even when the family might be the problem. The long-
term solutions to child abuse are the same as the solutions to homelessness—
"the family." This emphasis does not protect existing children, if the family is
the site of abuse. And valorization of the family also encourages the creation
of a new generation of unwanted kids.

At the St. Francis Xavier welfare rights clinic on Sundays, many homeless
men discussed their strategies for survival. Too many of them shared George's:

> As soon as I get me those foodstamps I'm goin' home to my
> woman and give her a child. She's got three of them now but
> ain't none of them mine.
>
> *Why, George? How would that help you?*
> I might, she might let me stay, if one of them kids is mine. She's
> got the apartment from the welfare.

Wendell was a 28-year old man who had recently been released from prison
when I met him. He had never been employed, and was jailed for possession
of crack. Wendell explained his ideas about "standing tall" as he waited on line
for a referral to a city shelter:

> I be outta this soon, this here predicament. I got two little girls I
> ain't seen since they was babies. I'm goin' to see my girlfriend,
> see if I can't make us a baby boy. She don't want to see me, but
> I'm gonna make that baby and then I be standing tall. I been
> thinkin' about this a long time.

These men, fathers and sons, are caught in the destructive cycles of poverty, racism, and a gender ideology that gives them only one route to manhood—fatherhood. Many of them feel that their masculinity has been beaten out of them, either literally at the hands of their parents or else by their experiences of poverty and despair, and fatherhood sometimes seems a solution, reinforcing their masculinity while at the same time giving them a step out of hopelessness by being identified by the system as part of a family. As we saw from the experiences of other men earlier in this chapter, that route to masculinity might only work temporarily, but for men living in the day-to-day game of survival, permanence is meaningless, and unfathomable.

GENDER SUCCESS

In all my time of field research, I heard more painful and tragic stories than hopeful ones, but one man always stood out in my mind. That man was Ed Gwynne. Ed grew up in a middle-class family, went to college, had a career and a family before his son and then his wife died. But even those traumas, which shook him to the core, did not seem to shake his image of himself as a man. For all of these reasons, but perhaps especially the latter, I dared to hope that Ed's story would have a happy ending.

> Well now I'm into two and a half years of homelessness and how I became homeless, I always attribute my homelessness to my drugging and drinking. As you may know or may not know I started out in Westchester County and I have a degree in theology from Virginia Union University in Richmond. I came from a pretty good background, my parents were hard working, educated people. My mother was an educator, teacher and a principal of a junior high school, and my father is a Baptist minister and pastor of a church up in Connecticut, and so I came from a good home life, there was no abuse, no drinking, no drugging.
>
> My father was somewhat rigid, my mother was always on me about going to school, and keeping good grades and keeping my grade level up and my father was "you have to go to church and I want you to go to youth group" so there was pressure, but um, it was a warm and loving home. I had my own room and bicycles and a yard and dogs and I sang in the choir and was in the Boy Scouts, so all of the things that, you know, allowance and things like that, I finished high school, went on to college, completed college and came back and my father, I remember one conversation with my father about what I was going to be doing, he thought I was gonna follow in his footsteps and

54

become a minister and um, I told him, he said well you have a degree in theology I'd like for you to come and head up the youth group in the church. And I told him I didn't want to do that. He was very upset and I went on to work in probation and case aid and the neighborhood youth corps.

In Virginia?

No, in White Plains, New York, and then from there I went on to other things, got involved with a youth center and a youth group there in Greenburgh, New York who wanted to have a youth center. This was the late sixties and we started a youth center and they asked me to become the director and I worked at a little Tasty Freeze hamburger place to help because they couldn't really afford to pay me that much money, but I enjoyed it. I was involved, and I was involved in community work, and my father never understood, I went to church occasionally and stuff. And I got involved with a young lady and we had a son and we lived together for awhile and my father just really did not stand behind that. That I was not a real man. That I was living like a pauper, that "all this money I spent to send you off to school and you're not doing anything with your life."

But I enjoyed it. I was working in a youth center with about 500 members and I was making about five to six thousand a year and I was enjoying it, I was enjoying what I was doing. There was no drinking or drugging during high school nor during college. Drugs came late in my life. Um, we lost our son, he died, and I was young, I was twenty-four, twenty-five years old and she was twenty-two, and um, to deal with the pain I started drinking and doing marijuana. Most of my friends were firemen and policemen and we'd gone off to college and came back, so we were doing pretty good, whatever.

And nine months later Sylvia committed suicide, she killed herself, my son's mother, she just couldn't deal with it, she overdosed and she never did drugs. And some people said how do you know it was a suicide, I said " 'cause she never did drugs, she wouldn't ever." I couldn't, she wouldn't smoke pot and somehow she got ahold of some heroin and a syringe and she didn't know what she was doing and she overdosed. And I always said it was a suicide. And to deal with that I drank more, and I drugged more, and I got involved with cocaine and heroin and I never, I never shot drugs I always sniffed, 'cause I'm afraid of needles even now, you know, thank God for that.

Then I was offered a job in Yonkers, good money, being the
director of a an educational and vocational program in the
criminal justice system dealing with teenage boys and girls
who'd been through the criminal justice system who did not
have a high school diploma. So I was beginning to make sixteen,
seventeen thousand—in 1969-70 that wasn't bad. And I did that
for a couple years and continued to drink and drug and then I
took a job working with the Jewish Board of Family/Children
Services in Hawthorne, New York, and got involved there with a
residential treatment program. I began to move up the ladder of
success, making good money, didn't have to pay any rent, and I
became an administrator after a year, and I stayed at this one job
for sixteen years. I worked in group homes, and after a while I
became the director of the girls' unit, I ran the whole entire
girls' unit which was responsible for about 85-90 girls. I had a
staff of about 30-40 people, had a secretary, had an office, had a
beeper, had cars at my disposal, doing well, I was making around
forty grand a year. And of course I was doing drugs, they were
not advanced, but the more I advanced and the more money I
made the more drugs I did. Then I got involved with crack.

How long ago was this now?

We're talking crack, that was the last thing I got involved in,
we're talking about three years ago, I only did crack for about a
year. I was able to balance, matter of fact I became not only an
alcoholic, I drank primarily, boozed an awful lot, soon as I got
off from work it was either to a bar, or to someone's home or to
the liquor store to drink and to drink, and you know drugging
also but drinking was my primary problem, um, then drugs. But
as I said I got involved with crack about three years ago and I
did it for approximately one year where I was able to juggle, and
when I say I was an alcoholic I was a workaholic too because on
the weekends I would go work at Children's Village in Dobb's
Ferry as a weekend administrator. So I worked seven days a
week, but I always had my drugs, I had my coke, I had my
heroin.

*Boy, that's not usually the picture you get of a drug addict, someone
who's working seven days a week.*

Seven days, I was a functioning alcoholic and drug addict. And
of course you can't smell marijuana, you can't smell cocaine. So
I never drank on the job. I had sense enough that you couldn't

drink around the kids, the kids could smell that, but I always had my tin foil with coke in it, I always had my glassine bag with my heroin in it, and I wasn't one of those who'd just sit around and nod, it gave me energy.

So you'd snort the cocaine?

Uh huh, or you'd combinate it, you combinate it, they call it a speedball. You take heroin and coke and you mix it and you stir it up and you sniff it. Some people shoot it, as I said before I'm afraid of needles so I never shot drugs. Um, and I did that for a number of years, I mean we're talking ten, twelve years I snorted heroin and cocaine and could work. And with crack, it's what got me, I just couldn't function, I always wanted to run out and get a hit. If you know anything about crack, once you get it you don't want to leave it alone, you want to just keep smokin' and smokin' and smokin'.

And then my mother, my grandmother passed, who I was very close with, that was, I just went out on that, I didn't even go to my grandmother's funeral. The day that she, her memorial service was, I checked into a motel in Yonkers and I had about three or four hundred dollars worth of drugs and I just drugged out that day. Um, my father passed and I drank and I drugged. My mother became an amputee because she was a diabetic she lost one leg and then another leg. Things began to cave in on me and one day I, I didn't get fired from my job, one day I just closed up my briefcase, walked past my secretary, I said Goodnight, Dorothy and just never went back, and I ended up, I had a beautiful girlfriend in Yonkers and I went by the house and we had a joint bank account, I took some money out of the bank, I took some of the credit cards, I took her best friend also. And I came here into the city and I checked into a hotel, and what we call a mission you know the vernacular, the street vernacular it was a mission, going on a mission is that you just drink and drug and for like two, three weeks. And I woke up one morning and everything was gone. The money, I had melted down, what we call when you work your credit card to the point where you can't use it anymore, we say it's melted down. So I had melted that down, all the money was gone, all the liquor was gone, the drugs were gone and so was the girl that I brought with me. She got up and left.

At that point I was too embarrassed to go back home, I was too embarrassed to call my girlfriend, I have another son now

57

he's twenty-one, I was too embarrassed to contact him or his mother, I was too embarrassed to call my mother, who at that time was in a nursing home. So what do I do? I had to sneak out the back door of the hotel, I owed them, and I ended up on the streets and for the next two or three weeks I lived in the subway system, I rode the subway back and forth, back and forth, I lived in an abandoned building where I met some guys and we just stayed here on the west side here in New York in an abandoned building for three or four weeks, slept in abandoned cars for awhile, I ended up in the Port Authority here in the City for another couple weeks. So about three months I was on the streets, I got a quick education to the street life and being homeless and all of that but after awhile I got tired of that and I heard about if you go to the Volunteers of America down on the side of the Port Authority that they will take you to a shelter.

I was devastated with that, you know, I'd heard all kinds of horror stories about shelter life but I went anyway, 'cause it was fairly cold and I was tired of the streets and I ended up at Ward's Island, the Charles H. Gay Shelter which has 800 men plus. And I was there for the next five or six weeks and was involved, I learned a lot of things, I learned how to get on welfare which I had never been on in my life, I learned how to play the doctors. What we call playing the doctors is when you go, you take your Medicaid card and you go to a doctor and he'll write you a prescription of a certain kind of drug that they want on the streets, you take that to the pharmacy, they fill your prescription, you go out on the street and you sell 'em, get your money and you go buy your crack, buy your alcohol. So that's what they call playing the doctors, I did that for awhile, that was, that was while I was in the shelter.

So that helped me to keep my crack habit going, but then after awhile I was tired, I said I want out of this, I want my life back, I want to get out of this sense of hopelessness, a sense of no direction, I wasn't raised that way, I didn't want to live like that for the rest of my life, I didn't want to be on welfare for the rest of my life. I didn't want to be beating people, be stealing, I didn't want to get into that, I didn't want to go that low and so on Tuesdays there used to be some nuns who used to come, every Tuesday, I remember one in particular Sister Dorothy, and we would have what we call faith sharing, not necessarily bible study, but 30 or 40 men we would get together for a couple of hours, on a day like today we would sit outside of the shelter or either we would go into the dining hall and we would discuss the Bible, we would discuss our problems, our situation that we were in, the shelter life, and even our hopes and dreams of putting our lives back together.

And you know, after that, I met Marc, the Interfaith Assembly, the Education Outreach Program. I made many mistakes, many mistakes, in my life, but I pray I can do this, I'm a good man, I know it. So many good people have helped me, and I pray I can do it.

Ed had more tragedy than most people, but he also had, finally, an ability to believe in himself that got him through. That ability, I would argue, came not merely from his class background, but the way in which his class experiences reinforced his gender identity. Ed failed, but never felt like "nothing," like so many of the other men I spoke to did: "No, I never did feel that, I felt bad, understand, horribly bad, but never quite nothing." Ed—who, when I last heard of him, had been accepted into a Seminary—always knew he was a man.

"SEX OR SURVIVAL"

The Limits of Gender in the Lives of Homeless Women

chapter 4

DESERVING WOMEN AND GENDER RENEGADES

In a conference on homelessness in June of 1991, anthropologist Yvonne Lassalle described an event that had occurred a year earlier in an Upper West Side shelter. The women residents of the shelter staged a protest against rules barring visits from men because they were "bad influences." These women denied the need for the city's "protection" from homeless male friends, arguing, "we're not just mothers, we're women!" (Lassalle 1991).

A few days after the conference I asked a City employee at another shelter if she had heard about the protest. She hadn't, but she was not surprised. "It's a crazy thing to say, but sometimes their choice is, sex or survival."

In the last chapter we saw the traps laid for men by dominant gender imperatives. In this chapter, we will see the paradoxes of gender at work in the lives of women—subjecting many of them to incest and violence at home, and then "protecting" them by keeping them in their place—enabling homeless women victims to survive only so long as they embody the ideals of "Woman." In most cases these women will have options that are not available to homeless men, but some women realize, as those involved in the shelter protest did, that protectionism has a price. Regardless of that high price, though, most women eventually decide to pay it, for protectionism does allow them a luxury not afforded to homeless men—the chance to survive the streets.

In this chapter I will explore the ways women discuss their experiences of becoming homeless and trace out the limits that dominant and institutionalized ideas about "women's place" put on their options. In the period from 1990–93, I interviewed 178 homeless women. As with the men, I met the women in various ways: randomly in parks or on street corners; in women's and family shelters in Manhattan, the Bronx and Queens; through my association with the Interfaith Assembly, Part of the Solution, or other organizations with which I was associated; at the Saint Francis Xavier welfare rights clinic; and at a variety of other locations. Of the 178 women I interviewed, 83 described their homelessness as stemming from spousal abuse; 24 from child abuse (some of these generally younger women are counted twice, for they reported being abused both as children and again by spouses); 25 had been left by husbands or boyfriends; and 12 were left alone when a husband or boyfriend was arrested or killed.

62

Once these women and others like them become homeless, the choices open to them are, in many ways, indexed in the shelter worker's image of sex or survival. The virgin/whore dichotomy remains the centerpiece of traditional gender ideology, and homeless women are caught in its traps and contradictions. Because these women are mothers or have the potential to be mothers, they receive special treatment both by law and by custom—they are, in a sense, renewable virgins, sanctified by motherhood and taken off the streets. But while bureaucratic attempts at *purdah* reinforce traditional notions of women's dangerous sexuality, they only vaguely point to the identity of the uncontrollable other, men. Although all homeless men might in a sense be considered dangerous because they have failed to prove themselves as "real" and, in a sense, "civilized," it would be a mistake to ignore the racial composition of the homeless male population. These men are primarily black men, and they are, in addition, un- or ex-domiciled/domesticated. Without the civilizing influences of home and hearth, these men are portrayed as the most dangerous elements of society.

The experiences of homeless women deny this horrifyingly common conclusion. More than half of all homeless women are fleeing *domestic* violence, not street violence. The real dangers lie not in the streets but in the domesticating actions of gender and race, the ways in which from birth forward we begin classifying selves and others according to putative biology.

In general, the only women who remain homeless are the renegades of gender, the women who are wary of protection, wary of recreating toxic homes, and wary of bureaucratic condescension and paternalism. These are the only women who experience a gender crisis comparable to that of homeless men—women who choose to live on the streets must often disguise their gender to avoid attack by night, and yet must pander to public sensibilities by day to take advantage of the empathy factor. To be successful while panhandling, they must appear to be women, or even exaggerate their femininity, in order to appear "deserving."

This, for instance, is the strategy adopted by Letitia. For four years Letitia lived with a man who, towards the end of that period, became addicted to crack. He later tried to turn her into a prostitute by begging, cajoling, and threatening her. Letitia did not cooperate, and she was raped and beaten by her boyfriend and some of his friends. The men then left the apartment and never returned. Letitia is now seropositive for the HIV virus.

> See how I look now? You won't recognize me later on, in the dark. These are my beggin clothes, but when the people go home I turn butch. I even do that to get a meal in the soup kitchens, they's all men and I don't want no attention.

Letita survives, alone, in an encampment in upper Manhattan.

63

HOMELESSNESS, HAVEN FROM HEARTLESS HOMES
Domestic Violence

In this section women will talk about situations at home that led to their homelessness; foremost among these are domestic abuse and incest.

Sara had been living at a family emergency shelter with her granddaughter for about five weeks. Her road to homelessness began six months earlier, when her husband of thirty years left her for "a younger model—midlife crisis." Sara and her husband had lived in a $950-per-month apartment in Flushing, Queens; once he left, Sara, who had always been a housewife, could not afford the rent. Though her husband had earned about $40,000 a year, she said they had never saved much of his salary. Sara moved into her daughter's apartment in Brooklyn, but after a few months she realized that she wasn't wanted. "I was in the way.... My daughter and the man she lives with have a problem with crack cocaine. They know it. The children know it, too. So I took my youngest grandchild and here I am."

Sara was afraid that her grandaughter would face the same abuse her older grandsons received at the hands of their mother's boyfriend. "I didn't want the little one to be hurt, and I think my daughter would have been just as happy if I took them all. But I'm not young anymore, sometimes I can't even manage the baby." As we talked, we headed towards a bench in the hall where other women residents were seated. Sara stopped talking about her personal life and introduced me to Tanya. We soon got into a conversation about the difficulties of keeping the children who were living at the shelter away from danger; rapes were not uncommon, and one particularly violent one, of a young boy, had occurred about two weeks earlier. Tanya shook her head in disgust. "Some of these men, being with their own women ain't enough. They leave her in the bed and prowl around out here."

Violence is part of daily life in this shelter, where visitors and residents alike must be identified by guards and pass through a metal detector to enter. Many of the women who are here have fled abusive husbands or boyfriends, only to encounter other people's violent husbands and boyfriends in the rooms and halls of the shelter.

Brenda, who was introduced to me by Sara that afternoon in the hall, talked with me later about her decision to leave her husband four months earlier.

> I was down, lower than low. Ten years, scared to go out, scared he'd beat me when he got home if one little thing upset him. It could be anything, you never knew. Sometimes nothing would bother him, sometimes not having dinner ready was enough. He put me in the hospital sometimes, I had broken arms, ribs, stitches in more places than I can tell you.

64

> *How did you finally leave?*
>
> I don't know. One day I thought, now nothing could be worse than this, not even being homeless. So I packed one morning, waited for [my son] to get home from school, and went right down to the emergency services. It didn't scare me none. I been through worse than this.

Brenda's reasoning, that homelessness would not be worse than the abuse she experienced at home, was shared by many women in her situation. Twan, originally from Brooklyn but now living with her son in a room down the hall from Sara's, described her own struggles with two generations of violence, and shared many of Sara's thoughts.

> One thing I still can't figure, is the world a violent place or is it me? Growing up, mama married two alcoholics, one after the other, the home was nasty. My brother and me'd be beaten a lot, the belt, slapped on the side of the head, sometimes I seen stars.
>   I went and got pregnant young, married the same damn kinda guy, short fuse, no fuse. He was drugging when I married

him, but nothin' like later on. And me and my son, we just stayed outta his way.

A couple of my girlfriends had the same problem, well almost as bad, and one day Maria's sister, she was like a social worker or somethin', she said, "You're moving out, girl, that's all there is to say." She said to me, "Twan, if you know what's good for you you'd pack your things and come too." So I did, I packed some clothes and moved into Maria's sister's.

I stayed there a few weeks, then he found us, threatened everybody in the whole damn building if we didn't come home, so I came here, thinking maybe he won't find us in the city.

And I don't regret it, not one bit. Well, sometimes I miss it, but you get a lot of support here, some of the people working here is good people, helpin' us, and I made more friends here than I ever had in my life.

The image I often got of "home" in talking to homeless women like Twan was not a pretty place, but it was still somewhat shocking to hear the details of the better life that these bleak, infested, and dangerous shelters afforded—support, friendship, and the chance to start over, to live a life without abuse. Jackie, who was living in a women's shelter on the west side of the City, had experiences similar to Twan's, both of home and of homelessness.

65

My husband and I fought all the time, all the time we was married. He drank and beat me, weekends the worst. One day I said no fuckin' more. Here I am afraid to have friends, ashamed of my life, what could be worse than this? Not being homeless, anyway. Now I'm getting someplace. I'm getting back on my feet and taking care of myself.

Jackie, Twan, and Brenda decided upon homelessness as the lesser of two evils. For other homeless women, the abuse, both sexual and physical, was inflicted by parents and other adults on them as young girls. For these women, the process of becoming homeless seemed to begin in childhood, the abuse constraining their life chances from then on. In the last chapter we saw men who suffered abuse as children describe it in terms of feeling as if they had "always been homeless" (and relatedly, as emasculated). Women who suffered sexual or physical abuse as children do not similarly describe undermined gender identities, but some of them did describe reactions in terms of their sexuality, whether in terms of avoiding relationships entirely and living alone, by choosing to be lesbian, by prostitution, or by some combination of these, as in the case of Jean.

Jean was 41-years-old when I met her on a Sunday in late April, 1991; she was panhandling on the southeast corner of Fifth Avenue and Tenth Street, leaning against the corner of an apartment house. She was thin and small, and said that the presence of a doorman a few feet away helped her feel safe. After we spoke for awhile, I asked if I could interview her on tape, and she agreed. I walked the seven blocks home to get my tape recorder, and we reunited and walked to a little health food cafe on Eighth Street. I paid for her meal and later gave her twenty dollars for the interview. Jean never told me her last name and did not want to leave a phone number where I could reach her. I lost track of her about two weeks after this interview.

In a manner of speaking I think I've always been homeless, quote unquote, for all of my life. The reason for that being that obviously I came from parents but I came from parents who didn't want me. My parents … I have to really start way back and give you a synopsis so you'll understand.

I was born an only child; my parents were affluent, you know, well-educated people, they're not alcoholics, they're not drug addicts, a, b, c, and d. Um, people that have known my parents, especially my mother, feel that she is a sick woman, quote unquote. She did horrendous things to me when I was very very young. She was a dominant figure in the family, predominating. Umm, my father went along with anything she said or did. In fact I don't even call them my parents but I'm not gonna use names now so obviously I'll have to say mother and father. If she said jump off the ledge he would say which way, it's just about that bad. As far back as I can remember I always knew I wasn't wanted but I didn't know why and I always knew that I was extremely hated by my parents. I knew this from when I was very very young. I was a very intelligent child, perceptive, and I was always aware of that, that I didn't know why.

Well, early on, my mother would incite my father and because he didn't have an outlet he would physically take it out on me—throw, bang my head against the wall, smack me. That was nothing, that I was immune to. It was my mother I was afraid of, she was the great brains of the operation, so to speak. And what she would do is find these psychological maneuvers that for example you, let's say you're building bricks, a foundation of your life whatever it might be, a friendship, she would somehow ruin it behind my back. A teacher would like me at school and I'd be doing well she somehow would destroy that, every little brick I built she would somehow maneuver and pull out the bottom one under it. I wouldn't find this out till months and months later.

She got a job at a courthouse in New Jersey, I won't say exactly where, she started out as a clerk typist and believe it or not she worked her way up and became the chief probation investigator for child abuse and neglect cases. That was her position. Yes, um, so eventually I turned fifteen, we moved from an urban area, Newark, we moved to a suburb, I won't mention the name of the little town. And when I turned fifteen I couldn't put up with the psychological abuse any longer. It was as if every time I had a little degree of happiness or accomplishment in my life she would destroy everything right down the line. I was intelligent, I would do well in school, sometimes she would make phone calls, to my teachers, my friends' parents, everything would just get ruined and she would do it in such a manner that if I questioned it she'd almost turn around and say well gee you must be crazy to think that. And months later I would find out that she would pull strings and do all sorts of things. To make a long story short I ran away when I was fifteen. She used the running away to say aha, you see, something is wrong with my daughter. Now, being that she had learned so much about the legal system, what she did is she used a term called incorrigible, are you familiar with that term? That was the catchall phrase of the sixties. And saying that I was quote unquote incorrigible, she had me incarcerated for three and a half years—psychiatric institutions, diagnostic centers, you name it I was there.

I think I was supposed to die in the hospitals. It was like concentration camps, especially one in particular, which was a private psychiatric hospital. At this point too, I feel as if ... number one I hadn't finished school so all my dreams of education, now I've only had a ninth grade education, high school, I was sixteen or going on sixteen at the time; number two here I am developing this life story that I don't want because now I'm a psychiatric patient, I was like in jail, all for nothing, nothing I had done.

I was sent back to New Jersey. Well they had no place else to put me so back to my parents' house, and of course again I'm an only child they didn't want any children I was a total accident. Back to my parents' house, then my father back to the physical beatings, they wouldn't let me eat the food in their refrigerator, so on and so forth, I had to reacclimate myself to the outside world. I was nineteen, nineteen and a half. Eventually I managed to get my GED diploma through all of that, don't ask me how. At which point they threw me out in the streets, threw a suitcase at me, any time I did something positive, this is a jealous, vicious, I don't know what other word I can use for it, I don't know her reasons, I'm still trying to find out.

I ended up in the streets and I remained in New Jersey for a period of about six months or so. I had a young man who was helping me at the time who I didn't involve myself with in a sexual or physical way but he claimed he was madly in love with me, whatever. Actually I just wanted to be alone, be productive and get my life back together. But he did help me financially. I eventually started working part time at the Humane Society, and I was staying from one friend's house to another, this girlfriend's house and that girlfriend's house, their parents were very suspicious of me because they couldn't figure out why did her parents who have money and who are affluent just throw her out? Maybe there really is something wrong with her. So everybody was suspicious of me, I could never prove that really it was circumstantial. So I was here, there, everywhere, when I worked at the Humane Society I adopted a dog who had my life story. He had been thrown out, abandoned, he was totally traumatized. I remained in New Jersey for a few more months.

[Later] I went up to Buffalo. I was here there and everywhere. I ended up in Syracuse, New York. I called this young man who had helped me in New Jersey long distance said to him, my dog was actually staying on a farm up in Buffalo, begged him to come up, pick up my dog and drive to Syracuse, which he did. He remained in Syracuse for a few weeks and eventually he left because the kind of relationship he wanted I was not interested in.

And following that I realized that no one was gonna help me. I had no way to explain myself, I just had nothing. I wanted to go to college, I had medical and dental problems, minor but still that needed to be taken care of, I wanted to give my dog the best life possible, he was like everything to me, and so (now I have to lower my voice) I prostituted for ten years, and, uh, in Syracuse, and this is what I did at night and I started college during the day. I disassociated myself, yeah, I had fragments of my life. This was what I do at night, I'd wake up in the mornings, this was not what I did, paid medical expenses, dental expenses, paid for an apartment, tried to get through college as quickly as possible, and so on and so forth, and I did that for ten years.

I finished a two-year degree up there, it took me forever to do that, eventually I moved back to Jersey. I met people throughout my life along the way, but nobody really wanted any part of me. People would like me, but that was it. Almost as if my whole life had contaminated me, and I couldn't separate me from my life story. So people like drift through my life, they like me, they respect me, but that's about it. I'm a loner. I moved back to New Jersey, and still always had very little money, I was always surviving on next to nothing. Moved back to New Jersey, continued college down here because I had saved some money from the prostitution, completed my four-year degree, but I still couldn't get anywhere because I had no records, no way to explain my life story. It was like every year made it worse. Every year made it harder to explain to somebody else. Lived in New Jersey, barely survived, eventually I ended up in the streets going back about seven or eight years ago.

Again, apartments were going higher and higher and higher. A friend of a friend told me about a shelter, quote unquote, in New Jersey, a convent which will definitely remain unmentionable. I lived there for about a period of about five years. It was a déjà vu of my past, it was the most abusive place one can imagine, to the point where I am paranoid of churches and nuns. It was horrible. It was run almost like a black cult. The nun who ran it had an agenda of her own, and she would pit people against each other and take advantage of the fact that you were vulnerable and had no place to stay. It was not physically abusive … it was just the worst place to live. My dog was living at a kennel, so actually I was paying double rent, I was paying minimal rent at the shelter at this convent shelter and I was paying rent for him.

69

As I watched Jean push the contents of her falafel platter around on her plate, I noticed that the only thing she had consumed was a yogurt and fruit shake. I asked her if the food was okay, and she lowered her voice to say that she had developed an eating disorder over the last few months. She said it started after she left the convent shelter and moved into an apartment in Jersey City with two other women. She lived there only a few months; when one woman got married, the other one left because the apartment was too expensive, and Jean, too, had to leave. She has been on the streets now for six months, she said, and when I asked her what she did when she was not panhandling, she explained her strategies of survival.

> I live basically in the hospitals of New Jersey, the security guards know me, they know I don't bother anybody, they know I'm quiet, they know I'm not on drugs, I'm not an alcoholic, I keep myself clean, so I go to the hospitals and I also stay in a basement in New Jersey, the city will remain unnameable where the tenants in the building know who I am. So even though I'm not really allowed there, nobody says anything they let it slide. So I stay in the basement or I go in the hospitals to use the sinks and that's what I do.

Jean traveled back and forth from New Jersey every day to panhandle in the city. "I chose this spot very very carefully, I feel protected, the tourists around the village and the university are kind, and the doormen are always watching." On good days, especially summer weekends, she said that she can make about $20 an hour.

Incest

Janet "Cookie" Driver was also abused by her parents. She was also what she calls "the child of incest," and her life, like Jean's, seemed to be all downhill from there. Cookie is a homeless activist, volunteering at Part of the Solution in the Bronx, in the speaker's bureau of the Interfaith Assembly, and working full-time in a city-run drop-in center for homeless mentally ill women.

> I came from a little town in Virginia by the name of Newport News. It's across the water from Norfolk. I'm a child of the '50s. The South at that time was very prejudiced—let me give you an example. One day my mother sent me and my brother to pay a bill. Being the sneaky kid that I was I decided that we were gonna eat 'cause I was hungry. So instead of taking a bus we took our change and walked across the bridge. We paid the bill, and we went around the corner to a little place called—I don't know what it was called then but today it's called The Lunch Box. I was about eight-years-old at this time and my brother was about five. We went into this place and climbed up on the counter—it seemed that everything was big back then—and this waitress comes over and says "May I help you?" and I said "We'd like two hot dogs with mustard and relish and two cherry Cokes." She said, "Excuse me, you have to see the manager." So Mel comes over—when I first saw that show [the TV show "Alice," starring Linda Lavin as a waitress in Mel's Diner] I said I know that guy—he said "We don't serve niggers." I didn't know what that word was. I didn't know what "niggers" was. I'm

looking around we're the only kids in here, we're the only black people in here—I didn't know I was black I was told I was colored. Everybody's laughing, and Mel says "OK, but you can't eat 'em here."

Anyway. I came from a dysfunctional family. I was the child of incest, I was also a child of alcoholics and the grandchild of alcoholics. And I got, I loved to read, that was my escape, I learned to read very early. I used to talk a lot in class and they used to always stand me in the corner and they would send notes home with my cousin, I wanted to kill him, he would take it to my mother and she would beat the hell out of me and then my stepfather would take over, and he had ideas of his own.

I hated my life, I hated myself, I didn't know it at the time. I got married at the age of 17, I had just turned 17, but by this time I already had two children and I dropped out of school in the eleventh grade. I was in a lot of pain about the fact that I felt dirty. I felt it was my fault that my life was screwed up since childhood. After I got married I started drinking because my husband drank, you know, "one beer won't hurt you." I wanted to fit in because everyone I hung out with was older than me and I was supposed to be grown up now, I was married, I had kids, so I proceeded to drink. I oftentimes thought "hey wow, I'm an adult, I have responsibilities." Not that I could take care of the responsibilities because I was too drunk to take care of anything, to the point of, I started to use, abuse drugs as well.

Eventually this led to the disintegration of my marriage, I lost my house, car, bank account, I lost my children, I lost everything. Eventually I would pull myself together, I would get dry and I would say "I'm gonna straighten up." I went to the local college and majored in electronics because I was always takin' things apart and putting them back together and they would work and I never knew why. I called it tinkering but it worked. I was living well, I was working while I was in school, and I started stealing to support my habit. I thought it was hip at the time 'cause I was high. One day someone, actually it was the man from the canteen, he said, "we're gonna have to let you go." I had stolen thousands of dollars. I lost this job and I was totally embarrassed so I started druggin' some more and I couldn't concentrate on school and eventually I dropped out. I've had every kind of a job, I've been a welder, a carpenter, a butcher, a landscaper, I've patched rafts, I've been a dope dealer. I had a

71

disease, alcoholism and drug abuse. I couldn't function without alcohol and drugs. Eventually this led me to jail.

Jail's not a pretty place, trust me. I found religion in jail, I didn't have anything else to do, it seemed like the thing to do at the time. I thought, I've got religion now, when I get out I'll be a new person. The lady from the Bible school would say "Remember, Satan is waiting outside." I got out in November, 15 days before my birthday. And I got with friends who said "one drink, come on it won't hurt you." Needless to say I had that one drink, and the rollercoaster started all over again. And I lost my job, found another one and lost that, lost my apartment. So eventually I figured I'd worn out my welcome in Virginia.

I left town on June the 4th, 1989, and on June the fifth I arrived in New York. I had no money, nowhere to go. I had about $150 between me and my friend. I was so naive about New York I thought we'd just get a room. I got here and I couldn't even get help from the Y. These people are rude, I was used to southern hospitality. My friend had lost her bearings and we proceeded to walk in circles. So we took a train to the Bronx where she had friends. The next thing I knew she went to this friend's house and this friend told us to stay, at least for the night. Oh god. It was a crack house. She didn't know it was a crack house. I didn't know. This is where I stayed for the first thirty days I was in New York, and I was so petrified, I was too scared to have another drink or a drug. I tried to get a job, but I had no New York ID, no New York license. So what the hell was I gonna do?

So I got into an alcoholic treatment program so I could get on welfare, and it worked and so I figured I would stay in this program for a little while and get my welfare check and *adios*. It didn't work like that. After we stayed in this crack house for thirty days they decided to put us out. And then we were on the streets.

For Cookie, Jean, Twan, Jackie, Brenda, and and the many other homeless women I spoke with who were survivors of incest, child abuse, and spousal abuse, homelessness seems like their last chance at survival, because it affords immediate escape as well as what they hope will be the opportunity to recreate homes without danger—that is, homes without men.

Thus, like some homeless men, many women are also fleeing home, but unlike the men, who are fleeing what they describe as the obligations and constraints of breadwinning, women are running away from individual men.

Gender categories are relational; each term gets meaning in opposition to its other. Sociologist Zygmunt Bauman (1989) refers to these as prismatic categories. In *Modernity and the Holocaust,* Bauman argues that "Jew" is the archetypical prismatic category, its meaning determined in a power relationship to "Christian." He maintains that Christianity has defined itself since its inception in oppostion to "Jewishness," that throughout most of the last two millennia the category Jew took on whatever content Christians needed it to to buttress their own self-definition.

This same relationship is true with the categories of gender, but it is ignored in most legislation and interventions aimed at helping or protecting women. Because gender categories are so interconnected, it is difficult, if not impossible, to reconstitute the significance of one term without changing the entire equation. Definitions of men as bad influences, for instance, do not adhere to most men. Ironically, the men who are "bad influences" are those who have socially suspect claims to manhood—poor black men. Men and women live together not just theoretically but in daily life—women and men are each other's parents, siblings, friends, lovers, spouses, children. Legislation which tries to protect women does not change men, and by and large homeless women cannot and choose not to avoid men.

Anthropologists have argued that hegemonic ideals of manhood are dangerous to men; across national and cultural boundaries researchers have documented the continual ritual tests of virility that men must undergo to be considered "real" men. Herdt (1982) describes brutal rituals of whipping and beating in New Guinea, and Herzfeld describes a "poetics of manhood" (1985) in Crete, in which men sing of their virility and then must prove it by stealing sheep and fathering many children. David Gilmore has surveyed the anthropological literature and argues that in most societies men face three primary imperatives, which "place men at risk on the battlefield, in the hunt, or in confrontation with their fellows" (1990: 223). He concludes that while "there may be no 'Universal Male,' we may perhaps speak of a 'ubiquitous Male' ... Man-the-Impregnator-Protector-Provider' " (ibid: 223).

These deeply entrenched ideas about what a man is do indeed cause some men to suffer, as we saw in the last chapter. They also carve out a kind of left-over space for women to occupy—impregantee, protectee, providee. They also doom efforts to protect women, since trying to protect women without changing dominant beliefs about men can only be half-hearted in intent and will usually backfire in practice.

FACES IN THE STATISTICS

Not all homeless women leave home—some are left, often with children, by wage earning men in homes they cannot afford to maintain, and they are frequently without any means to support themselves. Danitra had been homeless

73

for three weeks when I met her in a shelter. She, like Sara and many other women, was shocked to suddenly find herself alone, abandoned by her husband and the father of her children.

> My husband left me with three kids. The oldest is eight, the baby's two. We moved in with my sister, but her man didn't like the kids screaming and crying so we had to go. She wanted us to stay, but what could she do. The apartment is in her name, so if he ever goes we'll go back. Right now I'm trying to get a decent place for the kids to be, and figure out some way to take care of them. I went to the shelter and applied for welfare, and everyone's been nice so far.
>   I was so shocked, I had no idea he was leaving. And he took all the money we had, he said to pay the deposit on a new apartment, all his utilities.

Lavonda, who has four small children, laughed as she told me how her husband left; she kept shaking her head, saying "I promise you this, never again, sister, never again." She had just been talking about how difficult controlling the kids was, and I asked her "Never again what? Children, marriage?" She laughed even harder—"The whole damn package, sister, everything."

> I tell you something, it took me some time to notice he was gone, like for good. Look, so many times he'd be gone for days, come back wasted and skinny and strung out, it took some time to see he wasn't comin back. We only barely got by with the money he did have, I won't say how he got it. Anyways, after two weeks I said OK, he's not coming back, let's pack up and get on line for someplace to stay.

Rosa, who was listening to Lavanda's story, was a young and nervous woman; she agreed to talk to me only if we met outside of the shelter, so that the staff would not think she was "a troublemaker or anything." She explained that she needed their help and tried to make the staff like her.

> I don't want to stay here long. I'm scared all the time, for the baby especially. She's only three, she loves people, she may just walk up to the wrong person here.
>   When I got married I thought life would be nice, good, I was 17, we got an apartment, Hector was older, he had a job, we were happy. Then the baby came, we were fighting all the time. He stayed out all night, yelling that the baby kept him up

anyway he might as well enjoy it. The next thing I know he's in Florida, not coming back.

In most cases of the women I met, the men who left them left voluntarily. But in twelve cases, the men who left were either in prison or dead, victims of generation-spanning cycles of racism, poverty, drugs and life on the streets. The statistics are staggering—as Mitchell Duneier, in *Slim's Table: Race, Respectability and Masculinity* (1992) has commented:

> Perhaps no statistic is more troubling and has had a more horrifying effect on images of black men than that derived from a widely reported study, indicating that 609,690 black men in their twenties are "under the control of the criminal justice system—in prison, in jail, or on probation or parole"—23 percent of black men in that age group. (1992:23)

Rita's boyfriend is one of the faces in the statistics, a black man who has been in and out of jail three times. He is now there again, and Rita wonders if she should remain faithful to him.

> Well twenty years is a long time, no sex, no protection, no father for the kids. And maybe he'll be out sooner, but the kids'd be grown by then, I need him now, to help us out. If I can get me a place of my own now, then I'll wait for him. Otherwise I got to find someone else.

One of the women left behind was Darlene, who says she "flipped out" when her husband Joseph was killed in a street fight. Joseph and Darlene had lived in the same neighborhood all their lives.

> I was screamin' and yellin', they had to put me under to get me to stop, I was flipped out. When the drug wore off, I decided to stay under, see what I mean, but with different chemicals, anything. I would drink and drug and drink and drug, I spent every dime, stopped paying the rent, the bills.
> My girlfriend took me in when I was evicted, she lived in the neighborhood, but sleeping on the couch, I couldn't do that long. And I was still fucked up, she was trying to keep her children away from that. So after a week or so I said thanks a lot, catch you later.

It's not just the men, however, who populate grim statistical and daily realities. All of these women are part of an unabating trend, the feminization of poverty. In 1989, according to the Congressional Caucus for Women's Issues (Rix 1989), 65.6% of women earned below the minimum wage; 70% of women earned less than $20,000 a year, as compared with 28% of men; 40% of marriages ended in divorce; and living in a female-headed household increased one's chances of being poor by more than 300%. In 1993, 23.3% of all children were living in households headed by women, up from 11% in 1969.[1]

The welfare state was designed from its inception to protect women and children (see, e.g., Skocpol, 1992; Wach, 1993; Koven and Michel, 1993; and Gordon, 1990, 1994b). And, as Piven and Cloward (1971), Gordon, and others emphasize, it was also designed to regulate the poor. In this country, so-called mother's pensions were built into the Social Security Act in 1935. In Title IV of that act, Aid to Dependent Children, a program was established that would pay cash benefits to mothers, primarily widows, who were deprived of their husbands' support (Trattner, 1979). This program was expanded in the mid-1960s, in response to protests organized by the National Organization for Women against the exclusion of divorced and unmarried mothers (Sklar, 1993). It is now known as AFDC, Aid to Families with Dependent Children.

Today, AFDC is the only federally-mandated welfare program. Initially, the redefinition of "family" in the '60s was a feminist breakthrough: for the first time in U.S. history, social welfare programs were designed so that women and their children could survive without husbands, and without getting married.

But as I argued earlier, the convergence of protectionist legislation like AFDC with practices based on ideologies of gender and race difference has resulted in a situation in which poor and homeless men, and sometimes women, cannot survive as childless adults. Family members, adults with dependent children, are the only people qualified for AFDC, which is a federal program. At the time of my fieldwork, only twelve states offered welfare to single, childless adults. New York was, and so far remains, one of them. But according to a recent U.S. Department of Housing and Urban Development (1989) report,

> Even in New York, where virtually all sheltered families receive welfare benefits, it is noteworthy that, at most, 10 percent of all single individuals receive them. (1989: 56)[2]

What is happening here is that not only do Home Relief and AFDC target different populations, they also have different rules. The eligibility requirements and the duration of benefits for general assistance programs, like New York's Home Relief, vary by state and local district. In New York, anthropologist Anna Lou DeHavenon describes the nightmare facing a general welfare applicant as "Dickens meets Kafka." She argues that,

[R]ecipients of public assistance confront a world strikingly Dickensian in nature. They must endure both strict standards of eligibility and inadequate benefit levels.... People on PA face an enormous and byzantine bureaucracy administered according to a mind-boggling array of rules.... In this Kafkaesque world, recipients' benefits may be terminated even when they are completely eligible—even when they may desperately need those benefits to survive.[3]

DeHavenon's article examines the phenomenon known as "churning"—the administrative closing of a person's case, meaning that benefits, even if needed for survival, are lost. The rules for churning a single adult off the welfare rolls are completely different than those for women and children on AFDC. Childless, homeless men and women are frequently churned for failing to fill out questionnaires sent to them, or for missing periodic face-to-face interviews. Such questionnaires and interviews are not similarly required of people on AFDC; in addition, for the homeless, receiving mail is often tenuous and always difficult. In both cases, churning rules are efforts at controlling the escalating costs of social welfare, but the important differences in churning criteria serve to protect only people—usually women—with children.

The future for Home Relief in New York, and for general assistance programs nationwide, looks even bleaker than the past. The new Republican congressional majority has targeted these programs across the country for severe cutbacks, and New York City mayor Rudolph Guiliani is now proposing to phase out Home Relief entirely.[4] As I have argued here and in the previous chapter, it is not just men who suffer from these imbalances, but also the very people supposedly favored by maternalist laws and customs—women and children. As Ann Ferguson has argued, "women's mothering labour can either be a resource or a liability, depending on the context ... in which it is embedded (1989: 186)." In the context of homelessness, racism, and protectionism, women's mothering labor, central to their ideological elevation, enables them to survive. But it is also a liability, in that the boundaries of gender are policed by the system, and homeless women must behave appropriately in order to be placed where they "belong"—at home.

GENDER RENEGADES

Many homeless women, like the ones in the city shelter protest at the beginning of this chapter, have decided for themselves that protectionism is a mixed blessing. Some of them will initially resist its pull, but not many can persist for long, since the stakes are nothing short of survival.

Deborah was a young African-American woman living in an encampment under the overhang of the Coliseum on 59th Street and Central Park South. She lived with about ten other people in boxes and under blankets and news-

77

papers. I met her in the spring of 1991, a few weeks before the city planned to dismantle the encampment because of its high-rent and prime tourist location. I was walking by with a video camera, and she agreed to be interviewed. We went across 59th Street to a deli for some coffee, and then we talked.

Deborah described becoming homeless as "a way to solve my problems.... I was living with my mother and stepfather, and there was incest. I got to the point where I couldn't take it no more, and I went to a girlfriend's and never went back."

Once the welcome wore out at various friends' houses, Deborah, at 18, was left to the streets. Her first instinct was to ride the subways all night, but during one of the periodic crackdowns by transit police she decided that "life would be more peaceful on the street." She met her present lover, Tyrone, in Central Park and soon afterwards moved in with him, sharing his spot in the Coliseum encampment.

In the two weeks before the city's announced dismantling date, I met with Deborah five times. On each of those occasions she described the various interventions that social service workers, employees of the mayor's office, and concerned passersby had attempted—offers to get her into a women's shelter, offers to help her get job training, offers to accompany her to an intake interview, and offers of cash, clothing, and help with her appearance so she could interview for one or another job that the person knew of. One day while we were drinking coffee at the deli across the street, Deborah noticed a woman who worked at a nearby office building come to look for her. We crossed over to talk to the woman, who said that there was a job in the mail room of her building, and if Deborah wanted to she could come to the office early the next morning and get dressed and made up. "I'll bring makeup and a wool suit. What are you, a 14? I think my grey suit would be perfect."

As I listened to this kind, energetic woman offering substantive help to Deborah, my gaze kept being drawn to the men sleeping or reading in the encampment. No one had approached any of them in those two weeks, nor in any that followed. Although the entire encampment was highly visible and accessible, because of its location and because it had been featured on recent local television news programs, only Deborah was approached with offers to help.

But Deborah demurred, for reasons that were never completely clear. Her only response to me afterward was, "That's not what I want to do, wear her dress." I asked her what she would do once the encampment was closed down, and she said that she would keep panhandling until she had saved enough to afford an apartment. "I gotta do this in my own way," she said.

Jean, too, in sleeping in a New Jersey basement and washing in hospital restrooms, is surviving in part because of stereotypes of class, race and gender that guards use to decide that she is not a threat. But she is doing it, as much as any of us can, on her own terms.

> I don't want to get hooked up in the system, the system has
> done enough damage to me, thank you, they have degraded me,
> and instead of even saying My God, look at the fact that
> despite... and it isn't that I'm feeling sorry for myself or looking
> for a pat on the back. The point is, I still have ambition. I still
> have motivation. I don't want to take, I'm a giver, I'm not really
> a taker. I don't like panhandling, but I'd rather panhandle than
> get involved with the system and having them degrade me.
> Besides the fact that they resent me, see I fall between the cracks
> number one because I'm intelligent, I'm articulate and I'm
> educated. But I'm also out on the streets and I don't have
> anyone. I'm also totally alone in this world I don't have a family
> or anybody, so I'm like an oddball. They want to blame me, and
> say well gee you must have done something wrong, I mean why
> else would you.... The bottom line is, you know, I have two big
> factors riding against me, the factors are, no family, not one
> person in the world who cares whether I live or die, and again
> that's totally against me.
>
> If you don't connect to a family, it's as if you've been hatched
> out of an egg in our society, literally as if you've dropped from
> the planet Jupiter, do you follow me? And people can't
> understand this, what do you mean no family? And number two,
> I have no money. Now if I hit the lottery and had no family,
> that would be OK, or if I had a family and was poor, we would
> all share together to some extent, or even if my parents hated
> me if I had a sister in Ohio that would be something but I have
> nothing. None of those things. All I have is myself. So I built
> myself, again, I built my life, and I built inner strength and
> people resent that in me. They resent the fact that I survived. So
> I become more and more alienated, more and more skeptical of
> people in general, I'm afraid to be among them, I'm afraid to
> even discuss my accomplishments. And I want to stay as far away
> from the system as possible.
>
> Totally. I mean, all they do is degrade me—why don't you do
> this, why don't you do that, and you'd be surprised what I do in
> my daily life, things people would be amazed that a homeless
> person is involved in. And, but I don't walk around during the
> day, every minute of the day thinking I am a homeless person.
> It's like, I survive, I go about my business, and I do what I can, I

sort of fulfill my purpose in being here otherwise I would go under. As far as the system goes, you know, nothing is free, even if you accept welfare. The price to me that I would have to pay, I don't want it. I don't want it. No one will even take into account the fact that I want to help, that I just don't want to take, the fact that I did fight for ten years to get a college degree in sociology, no one will even take that into account. They won't help you go further, they'll help push you down in the other direction. I want no part of it whatsoever. None. None.

I could not find Jean or Deborah a few months after these interviews, and I do not know if their resistance served them well and if they were able to maintain it. Both women, and others like them, are in a sense "gender renegades," for their refusal of protection by the system is a refusal to accept dominant notions of a woman's place.

I spoke with many other women who initially tried to resist getting into the system but ultimately failed. Shirley was one of them.

I tried everything, staying at this one's[place], then that one's, then when I finally had to go out on the street I slept in the subways, the park, I was afraid of getting into the system. Everybody I know is on the welfare, and it done nobody no good. But comes a time you gotta do something, you're not getting nowhere sleeping in the park, so I said maybe they can help me, at least I can get a room, anything. When the weather gets cold you just get too tired to fight it.

Shirley had been living in a women's shelter for three and a half months when I met her, and she was about to be transferred into Tier Two transitional housing. Shirley was not only in the system, but she was moving up in it.

IMAGINED IMMUNITIES

Policing Public Space and Reinscribing
a Gendered Private Realm

Space is neither dominator nor liberator—it does, however, provide a context within which occur struggles to
dominate and overcome domination. (Bretibart 1984: 72)

chapter 5

ONE OF the most important daily struggles homeless face is for some measure of control over their immediate environments. Many homeless street
people poignantly describe their efforts to make themselves "at home" at particular intersections, doorways, or sprinkler system standpipes, establishing
neighborly relations with local vendors and merchants. The private lives of the
50,000 to 100,000 homeless people in New York are lived in very public
space, suggesting that we reappraise not only our notions of the public/pri-
vate dichotomy but also the idea of public space itself.

Over the past century, conceptualizations of urban public space and its pur-
poses have changed as dramatically as have urban landscapes themselves.
Frederick Law Olmsted, the nineteenth-century urban planner and designer
of New York's Central Park, strove to create public spaces that would bring all
classes and races of people together in pursuit of common recreations.

Olmsted's bourgeois utopia of ritual equality surrounded by actual relations of domination was in tune with his times: in post-revolutionary Europe, citizens were demanding that private royal gardens, like the Tuilleries in Paris or the Royal Park at Charlottenburg in Berlin, be opened to the public.

In recent decades, though, public space has come to be seen not as the last frontier of freedom but rather as a frontline in battles over social control. Since Foucault (1979) redeployed Jeremy Bentham's 1791 notion of the panopticon to describe a multivalent and multipurpose surveillance mechanism that could be incorporated into the design of built environments, recognition of the power inherent in spatial representations has led to a reexamination of the relationship of social and spatial organization. Theorists working within a variety of disciplines and political frameworks have formed a broadly conceptualized new field that Edward Soja has called "postmodern geographies" (1989), exploring the range of human possibilities enabled or constrained by location in and/or transformation of space. Some of the early work in the field was by critical marxists who examined, for example, social movements past and present in efforts to examine the social and structural causes of marginality (Tafuri, 1973; Castells, 1983). Others, such as feminist historian Delores Hayden, have explored the potential impact on social change that could be wrought by changes in spatial relations (see esp. Hayden, 1982).

This variously pessimistic approach[1] marks a distinct break with most previous conceptualizations of space in a nation in which space, particularly what was conceptualized as "open" space, has long been synonymous with "freedom". Throughout most of this century, even urban space was seen as a potential liberator, as Le Corbusier's grand designs for the City of Tomorrow ([1924], 1971) and Radiant City ([1933], 1967) illustrate. Corbusier's plans inspired a number of urban utopian experiments in the 1950s and 60s, of which Costa and Niermeyer's plans for Brasilia is among the more infamous (see Holston, 1989). The monumental failure of Brasilia and other modernist cities around the world helped hasten a Foucault-driven postmodern pessimism that primarily conceptualizes the built environment in terms of its concretized representations of power inequalities (see Garreau, 1991; Ghirardo, 1991; Rosler, 1991; and Sennett, 1991).

Contemporary urban historian Mike Davis goes so far as to declare that Olmsted's dream, that public space could ameliorate class struggle, is hopelessly obsolete (1990: 227). In *City of Quartz: Excavating the Future in Los Angeles* (1990), Davis traces the political and economic history of Southern California and documents the legislation, private decisions, and public battles that were instrumental in turning the urban sprawl of Los Angeles and its suburbs into a series of exclusive, often gated communities. This trend to super-segregation and gated communities that Davis documents in Los Angeles is, according to Reich (1991), a national and global phenomenon, as communities move to, in

Frank Rich's[2] terms, immunize themselves from the social dangers posed by undesirables.

But though this trend may intend portend our future, it is not quite the present, at least not in New York. No person, from any class, is immune from rubbing elbows with homeless people in Manhattan. Every bit of public space—from the parks of lower Manhattan and City Hall, the streets surrounding Wall Street, the midtown arcades and atriums, the libraries, Central Park, the subway platforms, and nearly every street corner from the Battery to Harlem—is simultaneously the turf of homeless panhandlers or squatters. In New York, the public still includes the people at the bottom, at least in terms of public space.

But this public is a gendered one: the staking out of public space in the city is a phenomenon dominated by homeless men. This is true for two reasons, opposite sides of the same coin: homeless women's fears of rape and attack, and the greater opportunities available to women under formal and informal practices of welfare bureaucracies. Earlier I argued that protectionist policies carried a mixed legacy for women: on the one hand, women, regardless of race or circumstance, are seen as potentially rehabilitatable because of actual or potential motherhood; and yet, as the protest in the city shelter I described in chapter four emphasized, some women are aware of the price of protection.

Dominant discourses that celestialize motherhood enable homeless African-American women to counter the social stigma of "blackness" in a way that men cannot. As real or potential mothers, African-American women seem to escape the harshest indictments of racism in a contradictory biological discourse: black people are inherently different, and dangerous, but black women are inherently women. Black men bear the brunt of this political semiotic that balances gender with race in determining social worth—they are aggressive because they are men, and dangerous because they are black. In *Haiti: State against Nation* (1990), Michel-Rolph Trouillot cites a nineteenth-century Haitian saying in a discussion of the social determinants of color: "The rich black is a mulatto; the poor mulatto is a black" (1990: 120). For homeless New Yorkers the apposite phrase would be: "The black woman is a woman; the black man is a black."

This is the opposite of a phenomenon many anthropologists have described in which women wear the colors, figuratively and literally, of their ethnic identity. Carol A. Smith (1995), for example, describes the gender politics of Mayan ethnic markers in Guatemala. Smith contends that Mayan women accept the burden of maintaining the symbols of ethnic identity, and are thus complicit in the reproduction of the dominant race/class/gender system, because in so doing they exchange particular freedoms for personal security within their communities. Smith argues that the trade off these women make,

83

in accepting sexual and cultural constraints, actually gives them the best position of any women in Guatemala, for they can inherit land, are relatively secure and autonomous within the community, and can seek divorce and mediation if mistreated by their husbands. Thus they cooperate in maintaining an essentialist, oppressive system, but they are subjects, not objects, of that oppression. This part of Smith's argument is also relevant here, because she explains, using something other than false consciousness, why and how people might participate in a system that oppresses them.

I see the situation of homeless women somewhat analogously: homeless women are ultimately complicit in maintaining and recreating the dominant discourse on gender and women's place because that discourse and its protectionist entailments gives them a leg up for survival. But contrary to the situation of Mayan women, African-American homeless women are not the ones who bear the stigma of ethnic or racial identity: those distinctions rest on the shoulders of homeless African-American men. In order to survive, homeless women have little choice but to be active agents of their own suburbanization, complicit actors in a system that defines their place as home and finds homes for them in the outer boroughs beyond the borders of Manhattan. The struggle over the Manhattan landscape is left largely to men, primarily black men who are childless or do not live with their children; these men are left without homes in part because they are seen as hypermasculinized and untamed, not belonging within the domesticated confines of home.

84

The movement toward what I am calling here the suburbanization of homeless women in New York City today is not the same as the suburbanization process that began in the early part of the twentieth century. In that process, male and female social reformers attempted to protect and exclude women from urban work spaces. These efforts met with varying degrees of resistance as some feminists, allied with working class women, attempted to reappropriate urban space (Sklar, 1973; Cott, 1977; and Davidoff, 1979) while others, particularly white, middle-class women, largely acquiesced and even actively promoted their own marginalization because it simultaneously reinforced their class status (Ehrenreich and English, 1978; Hayden, 1982). For homeless women today the stakes are not class privilege but survival. But this survival is only possible with marginalization, and ironically feminist victories in the social welfare arena work to help women survive by reinscribing women's place—in the home and in the suburbs.

In this chapter I will trace out the human geographies of homelessness that are created as homeless people interact with, strategize around, and react against other New Yorkers' ideas about which particular kinds of people are worthy of help, sympathy, or housing. The differential treatment accorded to homeless men and women often consigns them to what Appadurai (1988) has called "incarcerating" spaces, but, as we have already seen, the nature of those prisons, and the possibilities for surviving them, are dramatically different. To paraphrase Gupta and Ferguson (1992), there is an isomorphism of space and gender in New York City that can only be understood with reference to discourses of race difference.

THE GENDERED URBAN STREETSCAPE

The interplay of ideologies of gender and racial difference is particularly vivid in the case of homelessness. Little in the lives of homeless men and women takes place behind closed doors, and their dependence on the welfare state is more direct than that of those of us with homes. The negotiations of homeless people through thickets of complex evaluative practices are more visible, as are the effects of differential views of social worth.

Women on the Move

During the day on the streets of Manhattan homeless women are visible, though not in anywhere near the numbers of men. Since the census figures on gender were not available to me that first year in the field, I conducted various studies with the help of three research assistants to find out how big the differences were. The results varied by season and by neighborhood.

On one day in February of 1990, my research assistants and I counted 24 women panhandling or just sitting or lying on the streets in the area between 42nd and 50th streets, from the East River to the Hudson. In the same area we counted 210 men. By nightfall, nearly half of the women were gone; we found 192 men but only 13 women. On subsequent days in March and April of that year, there were sometimes twice as many women as there had been in February, but relatively stable numbers of men.

In the area surrounding Washington Square Park and New York University, men outnumbered women by approximately 7 to 1 on the three days sampled that spring, but at night there were nearly 20 men for each woman. Four blocks to the south, however, in Soho, there were usually few men or women on the streets. In April I asked a cop passing the Greene Street Post Office why this was. "It depends on the street and the neighborhood. On some shopping streets, not only here but uptown, Fifth Avenue, like that, we have orders to move people along."

The next day I walked up Fifth Avenue and found that he was right. On lower Fifth Avenue, from 8th Street through the 40s, I counted 61 men and 10 women sitting on the streets, leaning against buildings, sleeping in doorways or standing on the corners. From 50th through 68th streets there were 7 women and 12 men, which is about half as many people as I counted below 50th street. But there were two other differences—almost all of the homeless people on this section of Fifth Avenue were standing on street corners instead or walking up and down the streets, and more of them were women. At night

I walked the 18-block northern section again, and found that the women had virtually disappeared but the numbers of men tripled.

Throughout the year I wondered where the women went at night, and during that time I asked many of them:

> I come in in the mornings on the 7 [a subway line running from Flushing, Queens into Grand Central Station in Manhattan]. I sometimes work the cars on the ride in, but not usually. You can't make anything out there, so I come here, put in a day's work and go home. Just like everybody else.

> My fiance and I stay in the Park [Central Park]. We split during the day and meet up usually for lunch or coffee if it's really cold. And then we meet at night.... We sleep under the benches, or in the bushes. We put our money in our shoes if we can, if it's paper and we can get rid of all the change. Sometimes we can't because some people don't like us lining up in their store just to get a five or a ten.... I usually make more than he does, and I keep thinking I oughta be saving some, but we don't have an account and we gotta keep warm.

> I have a sister in Fort Greene I stay with sometimes, but her husband don't like it. I have some friends I stay with but they be doing so much crack I try to stay away.

> At night I go to the drop-in [an emergency center without beds; people sleep sitting up in chairs] uptown, but this [53rd and Park] is where I make my money.

> I stay out here all night long, honey. All night long. I put on this big coat whether it's freezing or boiling out, and I sleep in the same doorway. This is a good neighborhood to me, the people know me and they look out for me. One time I was gone two weeks, and when I came back people missed me! This is a good location by the park and the police, and the people who live here won't hurt you.

The women panhandlers I met on the street were most often single, (that is, childless) women. Our conversations, if they lasted more than ten minutes, nearly always included mention of their strategies for surviving the streets, such as attempting to disguise their gender, as Letitia described doing in the last chapter, finding a boyfriend to protect them, or shuttling back and forth from the outer boroughs into Manhattan, which is what Jean explained in the last chapter—sleeping in a New Jersey basement, using hospital washrooms to bathe, and then taking the train into the city to panhandle.

> I stay out here [on Cooper Square in the East Village] with my dogs all day, and then some nights I stay in a door of the school [Cooper Union]. If the dogs are quiet nobody minds.

> I live out in Brooklyn with my sister and her family.... I feel bad about being out here, but this is the way I pay my way.

> I got a fiance, and when he's not around his friends in the park keep an eye out for me. If I can't find people I trust I walk to the police station and sleep on that block—so many cops gettin' in and out of their cars all night long.

> I wouldn't be caught dead on the streets at night. Even in the daytime I cover myself up. I wear a hat, gloves, coat, raincoat, anything. I try to make sure the wrong people don't notice me. [JP: "But how do you get 'the right people' to notice you? Who are they?"] The ones in the suits are the ones, or people like you who walk up the street smiling. Anybody else and I just look at my feet till they go.

87

At night most homeless women leave the streets. Even in the day, they are generally not as confrontational as many male panhandlers. This is in part because one of the women's survival strategies is to make themselves less visible, less of a target for attack. But despite—or because of—the far smaller numbers of homeless women on the streets and their strategies of invisibility, many of the New Yorkers who do give spare change to homeless people give it only to women. This is the same empathy factor that probably also accounts for the higher numbers of women in shopping districts where homeless people are generally hustled off the streets. Women panhandlers are aware of the differences and are able to use gender ideology to their advantage:

> I didn't know how to do this when I started out, and I'd flirt with the people, smilin' and grinnin'. But nobody gave me nuthin'. The less I talked, the more I got.... If I just sat here all day sleepin' there'd still be money in the hat.

> I don't bother anybody, I don't even make eye contact. I lean against the building and hold out this cardboard box, and people

give me money. I can make twenty dollars in two hours on the
weekends.

You make good money on this block. That guy [a man with one
leg who holds a "homeless veteran" sign] makes out pretty good.
When it's nice weather and I wear good clothes I can get $100 a
day if I stand out here long enough.

I'm everybody's grandmother here. They know my name, and
some of the guys at the deli bring me coffee and soup. This is
really home.

If it is women and children who keep the issue of homelessness in the public heart and conscience, it is men who keep it in the public's face. This they
do largely by default: they have nowhere else to go, so New Yorkers commonly
step over them, day and night, on subway platforms and on the streets. It is
impossible to walk anywhere in New York, no matter how brief the stroll,
without confronting homeless men. The relentless and overwhelming visibil-
ity of homeless men seems not to engender special sympathy for them but
instead hurts their chances of success in panhandling.

They're fucking everywhere, everywhere you go. They curse if
you don't give them change or not enough. I used to cross the
street to avoid them, but I figure this is my city too.

I give to women only. I walk out of the house with loose
quarters and I give them to women I see until they're [the
quarters] gone. Women should not be out here. Nobody should,
but women definitely not.

Years ago I felt sorry for these people, but not anymore. They're
filthy, dangerous, walking around with their flies unzipped and
following you for money.

Drunks and druggies. Who cares?

It is ironic and painful to see these results of the interplay of various elements
of dominant gender ideologies. The invisibility and seeming passivity that form
part of homeless women's street survival strategies are fashioned in relation both
to public reaction as well as the everpresent fear of assault or rape. Women stare
at the ground, or flirt, or act grandmotherly, and often are met with sympathy
and courtesy. If a man is passive he is generally ignored because of the sheer

numbers of other homeless men on the streets; if he flirts he is dangerous, and there is no equivalent concept of "grandfatherliness" to evoke kindness.

One black man I met used an exaggerated and cheerful courtliness to make his approach nonthreatening. I encountered him on a snowy day in March 1991. While walking across Eighth Street heading east, I passed a woman with three dogs sitting on the sidewalk of Cooper Square in front of her wheelchair. I gave her my loose change and continued walking. After crossing the Bowery, I was greeted by a smiling man who bowed from the waist and asked for spare change. "I don't know if I have any," I said. "I might have given it all to the lady with the dogs."

"That's just what you should've done, Miss," the man said, "because she's a woman and I'm a man, and I'm supposed to be able to take care of myself."

This man, like many men, had internalized the discourses of gender swirling around him. And while he seemed to be bearing the burdens with uncommon grace, many of his counterparts do not. The same discourses and policies that demonize and ignore men are helping to create increasingly desperate and violent men. This is not the result that anybody had in mind in attempting to protect women and children; it is the unintended outcome of what are usually well-meaning efforts to help.

Each day, employees of the Human Resources Administration drive vanloads of family shelter residents—primarily women and their children—to look at apartments. These van rides are an open secret; most people know about them, but the HRA never discusses them. Shelter residents contend that the people selected as eligible for apartments are favorites of HRA employees. This belief, whether based in fact or not, leads to an eerie exertion of social control over women in family shelters. Women are careful to act upbeat and deferential in their dealings with shelter officials; as Sara explained: "Every morning I put on my happy face before I take my grandchild and walk downstairs. I don't complain about nothing, and I make sure LaShawna is just as polite as she can be." Or, in Jackie's words, "I try to make everyone like me, that way I can be safe, and get on to something better." These women seem to know exactly what is expected of them, but unlike the women in the shelter protest, they have chosen to meet those expectations in hopes of getting help.

Gendered definitions of social worth, and their resonance with traditional values, can be used to appeal for help, and those appeals can work, on both interpersonal and societal levels. In June of 1993 I received a fundraising form letter on pink stationery from Rosalynn Carter. "I'm writing to you today," the letter began,

89

> not as a former first lady ... but as a mother. Because as a mother, I have known that special feeling of looking at a little child, tucked in, breathing softly ... and felt the wonder of being responsible for that child.[3]

Never once in that letter were fathers mentioned, although parents were. Mothers knew the heartbreak, the agony, the despair of trying to raise children in broken down and vermin-infested quarters. Fathers were absent. And, as we will see again and again, certain men are indeed being written out of the picture of home.

Men on the Streets

Throughout my fieldwork I was struck by the relevance of the work of Carol Gilligan (1982) to the ways in which homeless women and men articulated their situations. Men often framed their anger and despair in terms of their rights as citizens, and while women seemed to take a more personal view of their situation, they also seemed to be more resourceful in strategizing their survival. The latter can be explained, I think, with reference to the fact that women are given more resources to strategize with. Homeless men, on the other hand, are aware of their position at the bottom of every priority and sympathy list, and since they typically remain homeless far longer than women they speak with more bitterness and seem more willing to indict the whole social order in explaining their situation. They are also more willing to rationalize their violence against other people in terms of survival.

> Where do I stay? I stay right here. Home is where you hang your hat, and I hang mine right fucking here. You see the way they're putting bars on the fucking benches [a city program to prevent benches from being used as beds]? So I sleep sitting up, what the fuck.

> I used to stay at Ward's Island, but that was just like prison, people [men] getting raped and robbed and shit all the time. I'd rather be on the streets, it's safer. Some of my friends say we're better off in prison—three hot meals is more than I get here, man. But this whole thing is fucked. Better off in prison than on the outside. And they spend more money on you in prison too. What the fuck is that?

> I do what I gotta do, whatever it is. I need to eat, I need to keep warm. If I don't get it one way, I get it some way.

> What would you do if you was here and people walked by all damn day? ... Who needs a fur coat to walk to the cab? I need the fuckin' coat.

> See this baloney? I just got it from Gristedes. Put it under my coat and walked out. I don't make shit out here, not enough for

my three meals. But I get by.... A couple of times I robbed some friends' apartments, but I don't do that no more.

I sit here all the time. I'm on a permanent sit-in against this government.

One of the homeless men I came to know well was Robert Templeton, who specifically asked that I use his real name in talking about him. Robert graduated from the University of Michigan in the 1970s, and made a film on the problems of urbanization as his senior thesis.[4] Robert lived in the Union House, an SRO on the Bowery, and instead of panhandling on the streets he sold his poems to passersby. The collection he had when I saw him on the streets of Chelsea in April 1991 was entitled "5 Poems to Rescue the City! such as *from* those SUBURBAN POLICE who commit brutality against City-zens." Robert read two of the poems to me as we walked to a nearby restaurant after I offered him lunch. I then purchased his booklet, for two dollars. One of those poems, about urban space and gentrification, follows, in the layout Robert used.

> *The Builders of Condos, or Condo-Mania*[5]
> I am simply AMAZED at humanity's heart
> How at times it can be cruel and heart-less.
> Even as adult my child-like love does easily
> bruise.
> So sensitive, so crushed when Fellow Ones are
> ignored and abused.
>
> There are men/women only in 20s and 30s ages
> Sleep in carved up cardboard refrigerator box
> cages On chilly sidewalks of L.A. and N.Y.C. like
> babes crawl in cribs
>
> While across the street their bought-out
> brothers slave-ly lift up swiveling
> cranes, planks and cement to build rich homes
> for OTHERS.
>
> I'm simply stunned how some called humanity
> Merely pass by the homeless living in boxes,
> those pass without even a GLANCE or care
> They shrug that someone but not they has to
> live in Whirlpool freezer boxes so dared
> While those un-caring hurry to work to afford

dream homes, since they are obsessed
condo–maniacs.

I PROTEST the movement in American Inner Cities
the HIGH rise and prices of condominiums built
for suburbanites, designed to DISPLACE the
URBAN citizens already here. But don't think
that all I can do is scream in defiance against
greedy developers. For I USE psychic power to
help stop unfair gentrification. It's crazy?
I've bugged out? You laugh?… Moreover I
deliver orations at public hearings (not only
do I write and recite poetry) for the rights of
Everyone to have decent, affordable, rental
housing (if so chosen in a democracy) WITHIN
the present neighborhoods.

But at times I rejoice at humanity's huge heart
How Spring up truly warms and is NOT segregated
apart.
Even adult my childhood emotions are stirred,
so sensitive to love and joy when cemented we
up–LIFT COMMUNITY SPIRIT deserved.

I met a number of homeless artists and poets like Robert throughout that
year; none of them—not one—were women. I wondered about it, until, as
other pieces of the puzzle fell into place, the answer came, banal for all its
unexpectedness: necessity breeds invention. Homeless men have fewer
forums than women in which to articulate their despair and rage, and unlike
women, they will remain homeless indefinitely. Many homeless men eventually choose to anesthetize their feelings via substance abuse, while others, like
Robert, manage to preserve enough self-respect to channel their pain in
other directions.

It would be nice to think that the courage and creativity of men like
Robert would improve their chances for escape from the streets; the next sections will convey my doubts that this is the case.

NIMBY AND THE RACE/CLASS/GENDER NEXUS

There are twelve public city shelters for single (childless) men and twelve for
single women in New York. The women's shelters have a combined capacity
of about 1,800; the men's about 8,300.[6] In addition to the public city shelters
there exist special needs shelters for specific populations (e.g. mentally ill, dis-

abled, elderly) of women and men. Twenty-two are designed for women, and eleven for men. For families (any adult with dependent children), there are about 38 private shelters, most of which are specifically designed for women and their children, and more than 70 shelters, residences, and hotels for variously defined families only.

All of the facilities for men are located in Manhattan, the Bronx, and Brooklyn; four of the women's shelters are in Queens, one is in the fashionable Park Slope section of Brooklyn, and one is at the United Nations School in Manhattan. There are at least seven family centers in Queens, three designated especially for women and their children.

Table 5.1
Population Characteristics of the Five Boroughs of New York City[†]

Borough	Total	White	Black	Hispanic Origin
Bronx	1,203,789	430,077	449,399	523,111
Brooklyn	2,300,664	1,078,549	872,305	308,798
Manhattan	1,487,536	867,227	326,211	386,630
Queens	1,951,598	1,129,192	423,630	381,120
Staten Island	378,977	322,043	30,630	30,239

[†]Source: 1990 Census of Population, General Population Characteristics, New York, Table 64

Table 5.1 shows the racial composition of the five boroughs of New York, broken down according to the categories used in the 1990 census. In comparing these figures with the siting of city shelters, two things in particular stand out: that there are no city shelters in the least integrated borough, Staten Island, and that only women and family members are housed in Queens and in stable neighborhoods in Brooklyn. This does not mean that there are no women's or family shelters in dangerous or run-down neighborhoods, but it does mean that there are no men's shelters in good ones.

The situation is similar regarding the siting of apartments for homeless or low-income people: in 1989, 59% of the 5,403 housing units built or in process for homeless people were located in just four Bronx communities, all of which had populations over 85% nonwhite (Brower, 1989: 117). In Manhattan, the vast majority of those units were located in central, east and west Harlem; in Brooklyn, about half of the 656 units were located in the heavily nonwhite neighborhoods of Bushwick, Brownsville/Ocean Hill, Crown Heights and Bedford Stuyvesant (ibid: 117). These three boroughs accounted for 100% of the available units in 1989; there were none planned or in process for Queens or Staten Island.

Most of these apartments are given to families, and city officials give two reasons for this: the large size of most rehabilitated apartments (five rooms is the average) and the special needs of families with children. But Frank Varde

93

of the City Planning office pointed to the media, and the public, in defense of the city's efforts. "If you leave families with children sleeping on a desk in an office [as was happening in the winter of 1992], the media will have a feeding frenzy. They wouldn't react the same way if it were a group of men....The media, and their readers, will react differently to a 5-year-old kid sleeping on a desk than a Vietnam vet. We all know single women will get better treatment than men, you feel sorrier for them. Remember the uproar when that woman was sleeping on a grate on Second Avenue and the Sixties during the Koch administration? The media and the public were outraged. Who's outraged by homeless men sleeping on grates? The city can only do what its people want, especially when resources are limited. The city moves from media crisis to media crisis."

City officials are not the only participants in decisions about the location of shelter facilities and low-income housing. These battles usually involve community boards, elected officials, neighborhood residents and often even potential homeless clients, and these groups do not typically agree on two basic questions: the characteristics of a so-called stable neighborhood (often merely a euphemism for nonwhite in the media and to elected officials), or the means with which to stabilize a problem neighborhood. These differences and others will become clear in the two case studies that follow.

Homeless People and Hazardous Waste

One of the most powerful forces at work in determining shelter sites is NIMBY—the "not in my backyard" sentiment that has gained unprecedented political clout in the last decade. Protests against homeless shelters, AIDS residences, and drug rehab centers are frequent in New York, and angry residents wield considerably more political clout than do their vulnerable counterparts. Across the nation NIMBY has gained currency as the rallying cry of groups with diverse political agendas in battles against hazardous waste facilities, bus terminals, gas pipelines, and incinerators. "This is the age of the NIMBY," declared the *New York Times* in 1988. "Developers of everything from hotel and airport extensions to soup kitchens and McDonald's restaurants have met the NIMBY squads. NIMBYs were behind the decision last month to close the completed Shoreham nuclear power plant on Long island. And last summer [1987], NIMBYs in six states and three countries kept the celebrated garbage barge searching for a willing port for 102 days."[7]

Many analysts in New York attribute the rise in NIMBYism to the experiences of the Love Canal neighborhood in upstate New York ten years ago.[8] Love Canal was situated near a chemical dump owned by Hooper Chemicals, a subsidiary of the Occidental Petroleum Corporation, and following a rash of mysterious illnesses among their children, residents suspected that toxic refinery chemicals were responsible. Their battles against Occidental and the federal government eventually led to a federal buyout and evacuation of the area, and inaugurated, some local observers claim, a new era of suspicion of industry and government. But other politicians and neighborhood activists link NIMBY to 1960s anti-Vietnam war and civil rights activism. "That's where the real mistrust began," claimed Margot Lewitin, a long-time community organizer.

According to a study by Cerrell Associates (1984) commissioned by the California Waste Management Board, the people least likely to oppose development projects are older, rural, Catholic Republican farmers. Young and middle-aged housewives and professional people with college educations from urban areas in the Northeast or California are described as the most likely to resist.

Part of the NIMBY paradox is that hazardous waste dumps and homeless shelters are fought in the same terms, by some of the same people, and over the same stakes. The politics of the left and right converge in keeping "public enemies" away from private property. Time and again, in accounts of NIMBY campaigns across the country, whether against group homes for the disabled, hazardous waste facilities, homeless shelters, or hospices, to name a few examples, the discourse of invasion typically ends up using the same trump card: the safety of women and children.

In late 1991 fears about homeless people erupted when New York's Mayor Dinkins announced a new homeless initiative—a program that would scatter 24 small shelters throughout the five boroughs. Reaction was swift and vicious; the head of the City Council, Peter Vallone, castigated the mayor personally: "You're unnecessarily frightening all of the people of this city and it doesn't make any sense. It's spreading homelessness and hopelessness throughout. It's almost as if you're saying we have a serious disease and we'll spread it so everybody will suffer from it."[9] Mayor Dinkins abandoned the proposals before the year was out.

But as I discovered as I interviewed people in two different New York neighborhoods, while for some types of neighborhoods an influx of homeless people is perceived as a problem, other neighborhoods actively solicit housing for the homeless as part of a solution to local problems.

Homeless People as a Problem

Briarwood, in Queens, a small neighborhood of apartment buildings mixed with single-family brick houses, is a sort of buffer zone: it sits between the middle- and upper-middle-class Forest Hills/Kew Gardens district, and the embattled neighborhoods of Jamaica near Kennedy Airport. In 1987, the neighborhood united to fight city plans to build a family shelter in Briarwood on Union Turnpike. Residents raised nearly $100,000 for a war chest, and they took their case against the city to court. Their suit wound through the court system until it landed on the docket of the New York State Court of Appeals, which ultimately ruled in favor of the city.

Immediately following the ruling, Briarwood residents protested, some wearing black to demonstrate the impending death of the neighborhood. But when plans for the shelter began to be drawn, many of the people who had actively opposed the shelter decided to become just as active in their efforts to make it work. The shelter, scheduled to open in late 1992, would consist of apartments for homeless families; Briarwood residents successfully petitioned for a small reduction in the number of apartments so that on-site day care could be provided. Because of community efforts, programs were quickly in place for on-site computer training, cultural events, and after-school programs. This transitional housing shelter would by no means be a family emergency shelter, like the forbidding and dangerous shelter discussed earlier.

In late 1990 I went to Briarwood and interviewed a dozen residents. Some of these people had been actively involved in the battle over the site, others had remained on the sidelines.

"I feel for these people, but my kids come first," explained Lorraine, a housewife. "We've been here for nine years. We work hard to have a decent life. And now they want to put drug addicts and crazy people next door. How can I let the kids walk home from school? How can I let them play outside and have a minute's peace?"

When I replied that the proposal was for a homeless shelter, not a drug rehab center, Mike, her husband, was unmoved. "Nobody has to be homeless in this country. You just have to want to work. These people are basically good for nothing. Either that or they're nuts." Paul, Mike's friend, agreed.

Elaine, a community organizer, expressed sympathy for the plight of homeless people. "But," she argued, "the issue is safety. Pure and simple. These people have no money, no jobs, no nothing. They do nothing all day long. We work, our houses just sit there, sitting ducks. Then the kids come home from school, what happens? How can our rights be protected? How is this fair?"

Safety, of children and of property, was the main concern of every woman I met, even though some had decided like Rebecca to wait and see. "It could work, and I would be the first to jump up and down." Two of the men I spoke with lived alone, and they both felt that safety was not an immediate concern. Property values were. Fred said, "If this works, great. But will the city really maintain the quality of the place? They don't inspire a lot of confidence."

Not everyone saw every homeless person as equally dangerous. Two of the men I spoke to said that although they were opposed to any kind of shelter, a residence for families was the most palatable option. Mort, who lived in the area for thirty-five years, said, "The way I understand it, there will be mostly women and children here. I'm still not crazy about it, because the men always follow. But maybe with women they'll know enough to be careful." Harold, a bank teller, agreed; he thought women "would be happy to get a new lease on life, and maybe they could fit in with the community." And when I asked the other people I talked with if particular homeless populations were more palatable than others, most people concurred. As Elaine said, "the point is, this is a family shelter and this is a family neighborhood."

Homeless People as the Solution

Not all neighborhoods campaign against housing homeless people in their midst, but the demographic predictors isolated by the Cerrell Associates' study discussed in the last section do not seem to apply. The communities of the northwest Bronx provide an interesting counterpoint to Briarwood.

In the Bronx in April of 1990 I attended a meeting of the Northwest Bronx Community and Clergy Coalition. The meeting was called to present community demands to Mayor Dinkins, who was scheduled to attend. The St. Philip Neri church basement was packed, and even before the meeting started I sensed that something here was different—signs placed on the walls and ceiling indexed a different enemy than the homeless predators feared in Queens. "Landlords are like dinosaurs—too big to survive," declared one poster, while the other depicted the huge arms of a cigar-smoking landlord, squeezing the life out of apartment buildings, while residents screamed "help" from the rooftops. It was captioned "Freddie Mac Over$tuff$ Him."

The meeting began about 30 minutes late, with no word or sign from City Hall. Organizers and community members were disappointed but hardly surprised. The theme was one of inclusion; the first announcement pointed to translation stations in the back if anyone did not speak English or understand what was being discussed. People Power awards were given out to members of the ten neighborhood committees that comprised the district, and the platforms of each neighborhood were presented in the Mayor's absence. The demands were for neighborhood security, day care, parks, community gardens, and housing for the homeless. The enemy was unresponsive government. "We need what we need for our neighborhood, and not what an agency tells us we need. We need HPD [the department of Housing Preservation and Development] to prioritize formerly homeless families."

The ethnic and economic composition of the neighborhoods of the Northwest Bronx is mixed. Some of the northernmost neighborhoods along Mosholu Parkway and in Kingsbridge have been solidly middle-class and significantly white for decades, while others, especially Bedford and Crotona Park, are barely viable as communities because of the existence of burnt-out, abandoned apartment buildings and vacant, debris-filled lots on every block. If this were the Los Angeles described by Mike Davis, the middle-class northern communities would most emphatically not belong to the same coalition as the burned-out neighborhoods towards the south. They would incorporate into new towns with new names and hire private security guards to keep unwanted neighbors away. But this was not what was happening in the Bronx.

97

The woman I sat next to was Rita, from Mosholu Parkway. She explained her position to me once she realized that I was taping the session. "Any one of us could be homeless, it's just a paycheck away. These families deserve our support, and we want the abandoned buildings in the Bronx fixed up for them.... The Bronx belongs to all of us. We're all united against drugs, and we all want good lives for our children."

Janet Driver, a formerly homeless woman and now an advocate for the homeless as well as an organizer in a particularly dangerous neighborhood, agreed: "These abandoned buildings make the neighborhoods of the Northwest Bronx unsafe. It's dangerous to walk past them, because drug dealing goes on inside. But if we get these buildings rehabbed, and move people in who care about their apartments, like they did in my building, then we can reclaim the streets.... The City hurts us more than it helps—spends its money chasing homesteaders out of empty buildings instead of helping get them up to code, lets warehousing of apartments continue when so many people are out in the street, and then gives most of its money to the gentrifiers."

Gentrification was one important focus of the meeting: residents charged that "Freddie Mac," the Federal Home Loan Mortgage Corporation, gave too much money to middle income groups and a relative pittance to families in need. Representatives of both middle- and lower-income neighborhoods at the meeting opposed gentrification, arguing that the solution for the Bronx was not to "bus the middle class in," as Freddie Mac was doing, but to find real ways to help people out of poverty.

These complaints were well-taken, but the problem isn't simply Freddie Mac. In an analysis of the city's ten-year housing plan, Bonnie Brower of the Association for Neighborhood and Housing Development in New York argued that "the City's claim that low-income families will be the primary beneficiaries of this housing is a cruel hoax.... Minimum-wage working families and other very low-income households earning under $10,000 have been literally shut out of the Plan. They will be eligible for only 87 new housing units (0.3%) citywide.... The higher the percent of minority households, the smaller [that area's] share of new housing" (Brower 1989: 1). That most of Freddie Mac's mortgage guarantees go toward gentrification does not point to a flaw in the Freddie Mac program so much as it indexes the racism in elected officials' quota systems designed to win votes and to make neighborhoods stable. The city's plan is to gentrify ("whiten") the Bronx to make it "stable"; Bronx residents demand that (primarily minority) homeless families be moved in to make their communities stable.[10]

Despite the differences in the approaches of city officials, Briarwood residents, and the people of the Northwest Bronx, they all agreed on one point: that only families can insure the safety and stability of neighborhoods.

Even homeless advocates, as we have seen, help to reproduce this evaluation. Andrew Cuomo's project HELP, for instance, creates housing for the homeless with on-site social services. But as I mentioned in chapter two, HELP concentrates on helping homeless families. Again and again, the rationale is that families are better risks because family members give each other more support. Single adults, in other words, need more help, so they get less.

THE "RADICAL" AND "TRADITIONAL" CONVERGE: REINSCRIBING "WOMEN'S PLACE"

In New York City today, race and gender are the battlefields on which disparate struggles for social and economic survival—whether in terms of stable neighborhoods, housing for the homeless, or the protection of children—are being waged. In most cases, homeless women, either alone or as mothers, fare better than homeless men. But at what price?

Belle Fox-Martin, a former counselor for homeless drug addicts, agreed that women benefit from strategies to protect children, but in our conversation she described the limits of protectionist vision. Fox-Martin argued that many of the social service people she encountered refused to see that homeless women were frequently as violent and dangerous as homeless men. She claimed that hers was an unpopular view: "If somebody sees a woman fuck up, they blame the boyfriend."

Fox-Martin's comment, describing the reactions of social service workers, indicates one of the problems that is a legacy of protective legislation—women are seen as passive and in need of defense rather than as acting, conscious subjects. The contradictions and paradoxes of this legacy for homeless women are particularly apparent in the organization of some of the semipermanent encampments that have been set up throughout the city.

There are hundreds of encampments, small and large, all across Manhattan. Encampments can be found in public parks, unused subway tunnels, and under just about any kind of awning or overhang. Some camps are transient and consist of nothing more than a few cardboard boxes and old rags; others have been organized into small communities of tents and plywood lean-to's that even tap into the power supplies of city parks.

The city makes concerted efforts to dismantle or raze encampments in high income or gentrifying neighborhoods. At the Coliseum on 59th Street, where Deborah lived, homeless people camped for nearly a year under the overhang of the building's second level, which sits atop a smaller, first-level cube. The camp was directly across from Central Park in a high-visibility, high-traffic area. Like the infamous encampment at Tompkins Square Park, the encampment at the Coliseum was broken up by City police in late 1991.

That fall I canvassed (with the help of Peter Malvan, my primary research assistant) ten of the encampments in Lower Manhattan. The large ones were in Battery Park, in Castle Clinton within the park, and in the Staten Island

99

Ferry terminal; the smaller ones were at various automatic teller machine locations and in the courthouse and jail plazas near City Hall. Women and men lived together in most of these camps, and in every case the women were identified as girlfriends, fiancées, or wives. Not surprisingly, in only rare cases did one woman live alone or with another woman in a camp. And while living as an attachment to a man is absolutely crucial to a woman's survival in the camps, the price is that women take a backseat to men in the establishment of camp rules and in the formulation of camp politics. This is the downside of the special attention accorded to Deborah at the Coliseum, for both dynamics are produced by the same social structures that simultaneously elevate and restrict women.

Perhaps the most famous encampment in the city was the one at Tompkins Square Park in Loisaida (the preferred neighborhood rendition of "Lower East Side"). The Tompkins encampment consisted, before it was demolished, of forty-five huts and tents which housed about 50 men and 15 women. The camp was a near-constant focus of escalating resentment among neighboring residents and the police since a riot erupted there in May of 1988.

The neighborhood surrounding Tompkins Square, represented by Community Board Three, was divided on the issue of how to respond to the encampment. Some residents wanted to reclaim the Park for themselves and their children ("there's so much human excrement in there you don't want to go near it" one resident told me; another said, "the playground may be fenced off, but look at what surrounds it"); others sympathized with the squatters and opposed the gentrification of their neighborhood. Camp residents were notorious among local gentrifiers and in the right-wing tabloid press for being "anarchists"; the *New York Post* suggested that the Tompkins squatters weren't "real homeless" people at all, but instead "radicals" from other areas of the city.[10]

The squatters at the Park did in fact espouse self-described radical and anarchist politics, and many of them were organizers of weekly community speak-outs, a variety of neighborhood films and events, and countless demonstrations (see figures 5.1, 5.2, and 5.3). A number of the Tompkins squatters were part of a steering committee that organized a well-publicized conference in June of 1991 entitled *Housing and the New World Order*. Press releases for the conference explained the links the organizers saw between the foreign and domestic policies of the Republican White House: "[I]t is no accident that George Bush pushed for the privatization of public housing in the same State of the Union address in which he cheer-led for the Gulf War. The millions more who will be displaced by his privatization/defunding agenda are to be kept in line by ever-larger police forces backed by right-wing courts. This is the domestic face of the New World Order."

Figure 5.1

Figure 5.2

Figure 5.3

In the planning of that conference, at which I spoke, women were indeed active. But they were not, with few exceptions, homeless women. The coordinators seemed to consist primarily of activist women with homes and activist men without. Whenever I asked for information on the politics of the camp, I was always referred to a man, even if the woman I asked lived in the same squat. One of the only times I got a direct answer from a woman was during the conference itself, when I asked Dori to explain what the symbol in Figure 5.2 meant. She answered, "That's the anarchy symbol. The top is the male symbol and the bottom female, we're bringing them back together."

If "bringing them back together" meant reestablishing patriarchal nuclear families, then Dori's statement matched my impressions. Although every person at the conference espoused ideas of gender and racial equality, the homeless women and the activists seemed to be cooperating in putting men forward as political theorists while erasing their own activities. It makes sense that, in a conference on homelessness, non-homeless women would think it appropriate to defer to homeless persons, but it was surprising that those persons were always men, and that female tentmates and co-workers of the men also deferred to them. This seemed to be yet another variation on the Haitian phrase quoted by Trouillot: "The men are homeless and the women are women." This is apt in two seemingly contradictory ways, in the situation of women in encampments, in which they take or are given a backseat to men, and in the more general situation of homeless people, in which the men will most likely remain homeless while the women, because they are women, will not.

These phenomena are not unrelated; they both rely on the traditional view that women belong at home, in private space, while public action, and public space, is reserved for men. And while this ideological precept helps to insure the survival of most homeless women, it simultaneously undermines the position of other homeless women, as in the case of the squatters above. It also continues to inflict incalculable damage on homeless men; witness the case of two men who built a one-room plywood "brownstone" under the Brooklyn Bridge.

Jose and two other men lived in that room, behind two sheets of plywood leaning against the bridge supports. The plywood was painted to look like a brownstone—bricks, windows, doors, curtains. I asked the men why they painted it that way.

"Well, this is home, right?" said Mike, a former word processing technician. "We wanted it to look nice, so that the cops wouldn't tear it down.... This is the place where tourists come."

"Yeah," said Jose, "maybe they'll see our house and wonder why this is all we have."

I passed this plywood brownstone frequently during the time I spent in New York. My initial response to it was to smile at its whimsicality and marvel at how "normal" the scene looked: one or two men sitting on the stoop, watching the world go by. But as I began to appreciate the nearly insurmountable problems that homeless men face in the city I stopped smiling, and by the end of my fieldwork I had to fight back tears. If women's place is in the home, as dominant gender ideology as well as social welfare legislation claims, the experiences of homeless people raises a question not typically conceptualized in terms of discrimination—where do men belong?

If women continue to be consigned to the private realm, when they become homeless various systems of local and federal government will intervene to insure that some sort of home is found for them as soon as possible. This leaves the public realm to men, primarily minority men. And while employed white men with homes reap the benefits of such a race/gender and public/private semiotic, homeless men, who are overwhelmingly black, suffer the consequences. Is the plywood home that Jose and Mike have the best one they'll get? Is this where men, particularly African-American men without families, belong in this society? For how long can the rest of us continue to try to immunize ourselves physically and psychologically from the nightmares that are legacies of ideologies of racial and gender inequality?

CONCLUSION

FEMINIST STANDPOINT theorists, who maintain that social realities can best be seen, and analyzed, from the perspective of people who are marginalized by the status quo, have recently argued that the standpoint of women is insufficient to produce adequate social theory (Stanley, 1990; Harding, 1991). What is needed, in Helen Longino's terms, is standpoint pluralism (Longino, 1993). This pluralism, however, has so far generally referred to the argument that it is impossible to understand gender without reference to the other positionalities that gendered people occupy in social hierachies, especially those of race and class. Feminists have usually left analyses of masculinity to male theorists, despite the fact that gender categories, too, are part of this mutually reinforcing system of power and significance. This study lends urgency to theortical calls for pluralism; it is time for feminism to put actual men, rather than straw ones, back in the picture.

Deeply entrenched practices of racism are argued today in euphemistic gender- and class-based discourses of family values and balanced budgets. These beliefs about racial and gender difference lead to theoretical and actual violence; today, "malign neglect" (Wolch and Dear 1993) has already claimed millions of poor black male victims, whose places in this society are few—in prisons, in devasatated urban ghettoes, or in shelters. As historians of the Holocaust in World War II know, genocide is an incremental process. And while the final solution may have been voted on by only a handful of fanatics at the Wannsee Conference, it worked because thousands of bureaucratic desk murderers, medical workers, religious leaders, and ordinary citizens took part, by action or by omission. When the atrocities of genocide came to light, the free world united in vowing that it would never happen again. Did we mean it? One look at the lack of meaningful response to ethnic violence across the globe, and at the homelessness in our own backyards, suggests that racism is as entrenched as ever, and that we must begin to reconstruct our ways of addressing it.

Social critic Derrick Bell, in his essay-turned-HBO-film, "The Space Traders," argues that we have learned nothing from history. In that essay from *Faces at the Bottom of the Well: The Permanence of Racism* (1992), citizens of the United States in the year 2001 vote for a final solution to the race problem, to send all of the nation's black people to an unknown fate on another planet. At the essay's end, millions of black Americans, forcibly disaffiliated from their continent of origin yet again, stand at the foot of Plymouth Rock, waiting to be beamed into the unknown.

In light of the bleak situation faced by homeless black men, Bell's science fiction scenario sounds a timely and urgent alarm. But how can social theorists and social activists best respond? It seems to me that the essential question for anthropologists in the 1990s is precisely this: whether the practices of anthropology and ethnography can be part of struggles for human liberation, or whether they are, at best, doomed to unwittingly reproduce relations of domination. The situation of homeless black men has become desperate, and an engaged and activist response seems the only morally defensible stance. The experiences of homeless people offer a radical critique of the economic and social organization of this country, and as an anthropologist who worked alongside them, it seems clear that my own work must be to help destabilize the race/class/gender status quo. My analysis of the ways in which gender and race are used to perpetuate homelessness—by insuring that only certain categories of people will remain homeless, thereby lulling most of the nation into apathy—has led me to conclude that the best way to begin to attack these injustices, in the late 1990s, is to avoid the language of gender and race entirely in social policy. This alternative, a gender- and race-neutral approach, was considered, then abandoned and even villified by feminists in the early 1970s, and for good reasons. But much has changed, and nothing has changed, in the past twenty years.

Given the current right-wing fervor to reverse affirmative action programs, it is difficult and discomfiting to conclude that it is time to move to a class-based system of redressing inequality, but I nonetheless do so. A continued reinscription of race and gender difference in order to eradicate those differences never made theoretical sense, and today it no longer makes practical sense. While I do not deny that race- and gender-based affirmative action programs have been successful in the past, it is the middle classes who have largely benefitted from these initiatives. From the standpoint of homeless people, racism and sexism have not been eradicated or even much mitigated. Athough some protective welfare legislation and feminist initiatives to ensure the survival of women without husbands have worked, they have done so at the expense of particular categories of men, the men at the bottom of the economic and racial hierachies—homeless black men. These initiatives have also worked to reinscibe the very family values that feminists sought freedom from, and, again, the women who are most constrained are those who are most economically vulnerable. A class-based affirmative action might logically turn these tables, for middle-class women and middle-class ethnic/racial minorities would very likely not benefit. But though women and racial minorities would not be the targeted populations of a class-based system of redress, they would nonetheless be overrepresented among the beneficiaries, for they continue to be overrepresented in the ranks of the poor. To address this situation directly, rather than through the mystifying discourses of race and gender, might well prove a valuable alternative.[1]

107

Ironically, given that class-based affirmative action is on the platform of the extreme right in this country, this approach would certainly be, in traditional Marxist terms, the most radical approach, since it would heighten the contradictions and inequalities of capitalism in the United States, the nation which is now the most economically stratified in the industrialized world. Regardless of the Conservative agenda in promoting this platform, this study has suggested that intentionality matters little in social policy, and that good (or bad) intentions can easily backfire.

I thus close this book with a most foundational of conclusions. Although the historical subject may indeed be fragmented, as many contemporary feminists argue, that fragmentation is functional in mystifying and maintaining the social and political power of the status quo. While social analyses must be capable of apprehending and expliciting the complexity of allegiances, performances, and positionalities that constrain and enable the lived experience of historical agents, responsible social analysis must also find its way out of the thicket of transpositional trees. My argument for a class-based approach to social inequality is a contingent and contextual one, one that takes into account particular social and historical situations. The concrete experiences, the human misery, pain, and despair of the homeless men and women I worked with provide, for me, a standpoint from which to argue that any discourse that implicitly or explicitly values certain identity-based categories of human beings over others can only reinforce those distinctions instead of eradicating them. Continued discrimination and differentiation of races and genders in the name of ending discrimination is no longer a viable approach in the social and political context of the United States at the close of the 20th century.

NOTES

Notes to Chapter One

I would like to thank Carol A. Smith and Regina Kahney for their comments on this chapter.

1. Watson and Austerberry (1986) first made this crucial distinction.
2. At the time of my research only twelve states had welfare programs for single (i.e., childless) adults. And since over 90% of AFDC families typically consist of women and their children, this means that 38 states did not offer any significant welfare aid to men.
3. In 1988, Alice Johnson estimated that men comprised between 75 to 85 percent of the national homeless population (Johnson, 1988); this estimate tallies with others since.
4. I am not naming this shelter because my descriptions are largely negative.
5. This shift from identity to performance is the most recent move within a general deconstructionist trend of the last two decades. Theorists from

various political and disciplinary perspectives (e.g., Laclau and Mouffe, 1995; Fuss, 1989; Fraser, 1990; Wittig, 1985; Irigaray, 1977; Moore, 1994, to name just a few) have rejected both the project and the holistic objects of foundationalism, including identity itself, arguing in favor of analyses capable of comprehending indeterminacy and the contingent postionalities each of us may occupy in particular situations.

6. Felicity Barringer in the International Herald Tribune, June 8–9, 1991, from a report in the *New York Times*.

Notes to Chapter Two

In this chapter I rely heavily on the work of Adorno (1987) and Jameson (1972), both of whom address what Jameson calls the prison-house of language. Adorno uses the phrase "the tyranny of terminology" to explore the "secret lust" that concepts, once posited, have for domination.

1. The National Coalition for the Homeless, Washington D.C., "The International Right to Shelter," 1989, p. 5.

2. These are figures published by the Interfaith Assembly on Homelessness and Housing, the National Coalition for the Homeless, and many other advocacy groups. These numbers differ dramatically from the 1990 Census figures, which I discuss below.

3. In 1990 the Coalition for the Homeless estimated the homeless population in New York at 70–90,000. The Partnership for the Homeless (1988) estimated the number at between 52,000 and 58,000.

4. There are many other classificatory questions that could be raised in relation to Census tables, but they would take this discussion too far afield.

5. U.S. Department of Commerce, Bureau of the Census, 1990 Census of Population, *General Population Characteristics*, New York. CP1–34, 1992.

6. The totals in this table vary from those in Table 2.1. City demographers suggested that the Census Bureau may have used revised figures for their gender tabulation.

7. Many advocates for the homeless and city leaders across the country have attacked the Census counts of homeless people, arguing that they are far too low. This is undoubtedly true: the national count of homeless people throughout the country is only 228,621—178,828 people in shelters, and 49,793 visible in the streets.

But despite what is perhaps a 90% undercount, I tend to be less critical of the overall effort, because, on one hand the 1990 Census marks the first attempt at any kind of authoritative count at all; and, on the other hand, the methodological problems involved in this first effort were enormous. Some of the problems encountered by Census enumerators illustrate the particular plasticity of statistics on homelessness as well as the deceptiveness of quantitative data in general.

In 1991, two researchers of the U.S. Bureau of the Census's Center for Survey Methods Research analysed the methods used in the 1990 S-Night count of homeless people across the country. The objective of S-Night was to "includ[e] homeless people in the census, rather than doing a census of homeless people *per se*" (Schwede and Salo, 1991: 1). The primary goal was to insure that homeless people were counted among area totals to more accurately reflect the population living in its borders and to insure that cities received approprate levels of aid and representation.

S-Night enumerators were sent to "preidentified" places, both shelters and street locations, where homeless people were known to congregate. In their analysis of the adequacy of the Census Bureau's list of shelters, Schwede and Salo note that "the Census Bureau enumerated more than twice as many ... shelters as the local experts identified" (ibid: 5). But they also note in the next paragraph that "[t]he local experts did not have much time to compile complete lists [of shelters]. The first local expert was hired just ten days before S-Night. Half of them were hired after S-Night" (ibid: 5).

Local experts from 44 district offices examined in Schwede and Salo's post-census study identified 868 shelters that did not meet Census Bureau criteria because both homeless and nonhomeless people resided there— e.g. substance abuse detoxification facilities, homes for unwed mothers, "and some transient locations such as campgrounds" (ibid: 6). Different publications of the Census Bureau disagree as to whether people in these facilities were counted as homeless if in fact they were homeless (cf. Schwede and Salo, 1991 vs. Taeuber and Seigel, 1992).

8. These results are generally comparable to those of Burt (1992), who found that single men were homeless for a mean of 41 months; single women for 33 months; men with children for 7 months; and women with children for 16 months.

9. For some of the most interesting examples, see Cibulskis and Hoch, 1985; Hopper and Hamburg, 1984; Hopper, Susser and Conover, 1985; Marcuse, 1988; Hoch and Slayton, 1989; Rivlin, 1986; Hope and Young, 1987; and Kozol, 1988.

10. Kim Hopper (1987 and elsewhere) has repeatedly argued that this pervasive image is inaccurate.

11. The first wave began around the time of the Second World War when researchers (e.g. Robert Redfield and Milton Singer) raised questions about the nature or character of specific cities and their relationship to a national "whole."

111

12. This term carries an extra-systemic connotation that would fit with a culture-of-poverty view, though it is intended to convey the opposite message.

13. Morton J. Schussheim, 1987. "Housing Problems and Policies." Congressional Research Service, Library of Congress, Washington, DC.

14. Keith Bradsher, *The New York Times,* April 17, 1995, p. 1.

15. Walter Goodman, *The New York Times,* "Critic's Notebook," February 19, 1992 , p. B3.

16. A billboard erected in 1958 in Los Angeles, for instance, claimed "It is amazing and appalling how many supposedly intelligent people have been duped by such COMMUNISTS SCHEMES as FLOURIDATION and 'Mental Health' especially since the AMERICAN LEGION and the D.A.R. have publicly branded 'Mental Health' as a COMMUNIST PLOT to take over our country" (Torrey, 1988: 89–90; emphasis in original).

17. Wagner, 1994, Marin, 1991 and Crystal, 1984 are exceptions.

18. *The New York Times,* July 26, 1990, section B p. 1–5.

19. The social production of these categories within "homes" also implies that the hegemonic family can be and often is subverted in practice, as more and more people in this country chose to live alone or in alternative families.

20. Schneider, 1972.

21. See Weston, 1992 for a provacative discussion of these issues in another context.

22. The problem with the concept of subcultures in the homelessness literature and elsewhere is that of positionality; subcultures are primarily used to describe the social networks of the poor. And while I agree with Wagner's affirmation of the findings of earlier urban ethongraphies, that poor people have extensive social networks and ties (Anderson, 1978; Gans, 1962; Liebow, 1967, 1993; and especially Stack, 1974), I do not see any heuristic or descriptive value in conceptualizing these networks as subcultural. In fact, my disagreement goes further, back to the cultures of poverty. The assumption is that the networks of ties, associations, acquaintances and friends of housed, middle- and upper-class people, who presumably embrace dominant values, are "cultural," while those of homeless and poor people are not. (We have allies; they have subcultures.)

23. The situation in Atlanta, where public housing is being razed to make way for an Olympic Stadium and where it is now illegal to walk through a parking lot unless you have a car parked there, is a horrifyingly accelerated contemporary case in point (Atlanta Task Force for the Homeless, 1994).

24. *New York Times Book Review,* May 7, 1995.

Notes to Chapter Three

1. In this and all other chapters, the names of most of the homeless people have been changed. In some cases, however, I was asked to use real names, and there I have done so.

2. Far more than 42 men in the sample were poor and of color, but the men I include here are the ones who used gendered language and the phrase "being a man" to explain their situation.

3. Ruth Sidel, 1992 has argued similarly—that men view their ability to take care of themselves and their families as an important barometer of their success in terms of both gender roles—father and husband—and gender itself.

4. As I discuss in chapter five, this dynamic is compounded by the gender-bias in the opportunities given to homeless women and men.

Notes to Chapter Four

1. Stephen A. Holmes in *The New York Times*, April 25, 1995.

2. U.S. Department of Housing and Urban Development, Office of Policy Development and Research, Division of Policy Studies, 1989, *A Report on Homeless Assistance Policy and Practice in the Nation's Five Largest Cities.*

3. Anna Lou Dehavenon, 1989–90 "Charles Dickens Meets Franz Kafka: The Maladministration of New York City's Public Assistance Programs," in The New York University *Review of Law and Social Change* XVII (2): 231–254.

4. *The New York Times,* April 20, 1995, p. B1.

113

Notes to Chapter Five

1. Tafuri, 1980 is perhaps the most pessimistic of the architectural historians and theorists, arguing that total revolutionary transformation is necessary before architecture can even begin to be liberating, while Jameson (1985) emphasizes the significance of Tafuri's work but presents a more optimistic Gramscian vision in his notion of anticipatory enclaves of counterhegemony.

2. "Sex, Death and the New Blood Culture," *The New York Times* December 7, 1992, p. B1.

3. Habitat for Humanity fundraising letter, June 1993.

4. Marc Greenberg of the Interfaith Assembly on Homelessness and Housing ordered a video of the film for Robert from the University's library archives; its message of the dangers of a future built on racism and redlining were painfully prescient.

5. At the time of my fieldwork, I obtained oral permission from Robert to reprint any or all of his poems, as long as I used his real name and credited him.

In December of 1995, when I tried to find him to obtain written permission, I learned that Robert had died.

6. This information was accurate as of October 1990, and was taken from the *Reference Manual for Food, Shelter and Resources for the Homeless*, revision of November 1990, distributed by the Coalition for the Homeless. These figures do not include the approximately 200 private facilities in the city, more than half of which are managed by the Partnership for the Homeless and which provide another 1500 beds.

7. William Glaberson, *The New York Times,* June 19, 1988, section 3, p. 1.

8. Ibid. But while the acronym NIMBY and NIMBYism might be relatively recent, neighborhood protests against locating commercial or social service operations in their midst are not. One of the most important ideological shifts that has led to NIMBY is, however, a legacy from the civil rights and deinstitutionalization movements: the belief that minority populations should be integrated rather than ghettoized.

9. *The New York Times,* October 11, 1991, p. A1

10. For an excellent analysis of the effects of gentrification on homelesss people see Kasinitz, 1984.

11. *The New York Post,* May 31, 1991.

Notes to Chapter Six

1. See Gilroy, 1987 for an important analysis of the cultural politics of race and class.

REFERENCES

Adorno, Theodor W. *Negative Dialectics,* Trans. E.B. Ashton (New York: Continuum, 1987).

Anderson, Nels. *The Hobo: The Sociology of the Homeless Man* (Chicago: University of Chicago Press, 1927).

Anderson, E. *A Place on the Corner* (Chicago: University of Chicago Press, 1978).

Appadurai, Arjun. "Putting Hierarchy in its Place." *Cultural Anthropology* 3, No.1 (1988):36–49.

Appiah, Kwame Anthony. *In My Father's House: Africa in the Philosophy of Culture* (New York: Oxford University Press, 1992).

Atlanta Task Force for the Homeless. *Misplaced Priorities: Atlanta, the '96 Olympics, and the Politics of Urban Removal* (Atlanta, GA: 1994).

Bachrach, L. "Interpreting Research on the Homeless Mentally Ill: Some Caveats." *Hospital and Community Psychiatry* 35, 1984: 914–16.

Bahr, Howard M. "Homelessness, Disaffilitaion and Retreatism." In *Disaffiliated Man,* edited by Howard M. Bahr (Toronto: University of Toronto Press, 1970).

————. *Skid Row: An Introduction to Disaffiliation* (New York: Oxford University Press, 1973)

Barak, Gregg *Gimme Shelter: A Social History of Homelessness in Contemporary America* (New York: Praeger, 1991).

Barth, Fredrik, ed. *Ethnic Groups and Boundaries* (Boston: Little, Brown, 1969).

Bassuk, Ellen. "The Homelessness Problem." *Scientific American* 251, No.1 (1984).

————. *Community Care for Homeless Families* (Washington, D.C.: National Institutes of Mental Health, 1990).

Bauman, Zygmunt. *Modernity and the Holocaust* (Ithaca: Cornell University Press, 1989)

Belcher, John R. and Jeff Singer. "Homelessness: A Cost of Capitalism." *Social Policy* 18, No. 4 :44–48 (1988).

Bell, Derrick. *Faces at the Bottom of the Well: The Permanence of Racism* (New York: Basic Books, 1992).

Bellah, Robert, et. al. *Habits of the Heart: Individualiam and Commitment in American Life* (Berkeley: University of California Press, 1985).

Bly, Robert *Iron John: A Book About Men* (Reading, MA: Addison-Wesley, 1990).

Bourdieu, Pierre. *Outline of a Theory of Praxis* (Cambridge: Cambridge University Press, 1977).

————. *Distinction: A Social Critique of the Judgement of Taste* (Cambridge: Harvard Univeristy Press, 1984).

Bradsher, Keith. "Gap in Wealth in U.S. Called Widest in West." *The New York Times,* April 17, 1995, p.1.

Breitbart, Myrna. "Feminist Perspectives on Geographic Theory and Methodology." *Antipode: Radical Journal of Geography,* 16, No. 3 (1984).

Brower, Bonnie. *Missing the Mark: Subsidizing Housing for the Privileged, Displacing the Poor. An Analysis of the City's 10-Year Plan* (New York: A joint report of The Association for Neighborhood and Housing Development, Inc. and The Housing Justice Campaign, 1989).

Burt, Martha R. *Over the Edge: The Growth of Homelessness in the 1980s* (New York: The Russell Sage Foundation, 1992).

Burt, Martha R. and Barbara Cohen. "Feeding the Homeless: Does the Prepared Meals Provision Help?" Prepared for the Department of Agriculture by Martha Burt and Barbara Cohen with the assistance of Nancy Chapman (Washington D.C.: Urban Institute Press, 1988).

Butler, Judith P. *Gender Trouble: Feminism and the Subversion of Identity* (New York: Routledge, 1990).

Caplan, Gerald. *An Approach to Community Mental Illness* (New York: Grune and Stratton, 1962).

116

Castells, Manuel. *The City and The Grassroots: A Cross-Cultural Theory of Urban Social Movements* (Berkeley: University of California Press, 1983).

Cerrell Associates, Inc. *Political Difficulties Facing Waste-to-Energy Conversion Plant Siting* (California Waste Management Board, 1984).

Cibulskis, Ann and Charles Hoch. *Homelessness: An Annotated Bibliography* (Chicago: CPL Bibliographies, 1985).

Cott, Nancy F. *The Bonds of Womanhood: 'Women's Sphere' in New England, 1780–1835* (New Haven: Yale University Press, 1977).

Crystal, Stephen. "Homeless Men and Homeless Women: The Gender Gap." *Urban and Social Change Review,* Special Issue on Homelessness, 17, No. 2: 2–6, 1984.

Davidoff, Leonore. "The Separation of Home and Work? Landladies and Lodgers in Nineteenth and Twnetieth Century England." In *Women's Work: Historical, Legal and Political Perspectives,* edited by Sandra Berman (London: Croom Helm, 1979).

Davis, Mike. *City of Quartz: Excavating the Future in Los Angeles* (New York: Verso, 1990).

DeHavenon, Anna Lou. "Charles Dickens meets Franz Kafka: The Maladministration of New York City's Public Assistance Programs." *New York University Review of Law and Social Change* XVII, No. 2 (1989–90):231–54.

Dominguez, Virginia R. *White by Definition* (New Brunswick, NJ: Rutgers University Press, 1986).

———. *People as Subject, People as Object* (Madison: University of Wisconsin Press, 1989).

Duneier, Mitchell. *Slim's Table: Race, Respectability and Masculinity* (Chicago: University of Chicago Press, 1992).

Ehrenreich, Barbara. *Fear of Falling: The Inner Life of the Middle Class* (New York: Pantheon, 1990).

———. *The Hearts of Men.* (New York: Anchor/Doubleday, 1983).

——— and Deidre English. *For Her Own Good* (New York: Anchor/Doubleday, 1978).

Eliot, William G., Jr. *Lectures to Young Women* (Boston: American Unitarian Association, 1853).

Feldman, Allan. "The Making of White Public Space: Policing, Public Safety and the Geographies of Violence." Paper presented at the Society for Cultural Anthropology Annual Conference, "States of Violence and the Violence of Status," New York, NY, May 5–7, 1995.

Ferguson, Ann. *Blood at the Root: Motherhood, Sexuality and Male Dominance* (London: Pandora Press, 1989).

Foucault, Michel. *Discipline and Punish: The Birth of the Prison* (New York: Vintage, 1979).

Fraser, Nancy. *Unruly Practices: Power, Discourse and Gender in Contemporary Social Theory* (Minneapolis: University of Minnesota Press, 1990).

117

Fraser, Nancy and Linda Gordon. "A Geneology of Dependency: Tracing a Keyword of the U.S. Welfare State." *Signs* 19, No. 3 (1994):309–336.

Fuss, Diana. *Essentially Speaking: Feminism, Nature and Difference* (New York: Routledge, 1989).

Garber, Marjorie. *Vested Interests* (New York: Routledge, 1992).

Gans, Herbert. *The Urban Villagers: Group and Class in the Life of Italian-Americans* (New York: The Free Press, 1962).

Garreau, Joel. *Edge City: Life on the New Frontier* (New York: Doubleday, 1991.)

Ghirardo, Diane, ed. *Out of Site: A Social Critique of Architecture* (Seattle: Bay Press, 1991).

Gilmore, David. *Manhood in the Making* (New Haven: Yale University Press, 1990).

Gilligan, Carol. *In a Different Voice* (Cambridge: Harvard Univeristy Press, 1982).

Gilroy, Paul. *There Ain't No Black in the Union Jack* (Chicago: University of Chicago Press, 1991).

Ginsburg, Faye and Anna L. Tsing. *Uncertain Terms: Negotiating Gender in American Culture* (New York: Beacon, 1990).

Goffman, Erving. *Asylums: Essays on the Social Situation of Mental Patients and Other Inmates* (New York: Doubleday, 1961).

Gordon, Linda. "A Right to Live," Review of *Brutal Need: Lawyers and the Welfare Rights Movement, 1960–1073* by Martha F. Davis. *The Nation* 258, No. 9 (1994):308–311, March 7, 1994.

———. *Pitied but Not Entitled: Single Mothers and the History of Welfare, 1890–1935* (New York: The Free Press, 1994).

———. *Woman's Body, Woman's Right* (New York: Penguin, 1990).

Gounis, Costas. "Homelessness and Institutional Control: The Ecology of Violence." Paper presented at the Society for Cultural Anthropology Annual Conference, "States of Violence and the Violence of Status," New York, NY, May, 1995.

Gupta, Akhil and James Ferguson. "Beyond 'culture': Space, Identity and the Politics of Difference." *Cultural Anthropology* 7, No. 1 (1992):6–23.

Hannerz, Ulf. *Soulside: Inquiries into Ghetto and Community* (New York: Columbia University Press, 1969).

Hayden, Delores. *The Grand Domestic Revolution* (Cambridge: The MIT Press, 1981).

Harding, Sandra. *Whose Science, Whose Knowledge? Thinking From Women's Lives* (Ithaca, NY: Cornell University Press, 1991).

Harvey, David. *The Condition of Postmodernity: An Enquiry Into the Origins of Cultural Change* (London: Blackwell, 1989).

Herdt, Gilbert H. "Fetish and Fantasy in Sambia Initiation." In *Rituals of Manhood,* (Berkeley: University of California Press, 1982).

Herzfeld, Michael. *The Poetics of Manhood* (Princeton: Princeton University Press, 1985).

Hoch, Charles and Robert A. Slayton. *New Homeless and Old* (Philadelphia: Temple University Press, 1989).

Holston, James. *The Modernist City: An Anthropological Critique of Brasilia* (Chicago: University of Chicago Press, 1989).

Hope, Marjorie and James Young. *The Faces of Homelessness* (Lexington, MA: D.C. Heath/Lexington Books, 1986).

Hopper, Kim James. "Taking the Measure of Homelesness among African-American Males Then and Now." Paper presented at the Society for Cultural Anthropology Annual Conference, "States of Violence and the Violence of Status," New York, NY, May, 1995.

———. "A Bed for the Night: Homeless Men in New York City, Past and Present." Ph.D. dissertation, Columbia University, 1987.

———, Ezra Susser and Sarah Conover. "Economies of Makeshift: Deindustrialization and Homelessness in New York City." Urban Anthropology 14, No. 1–3 (1985):183–236.

———, and Jill Hamberg. "The Making of America's Homeless." In *Critical Perspectives on Housing,* edited by Rachel Bratt, Chester Hartman, and Ann Meyerson, (Philadelphia: Temple University Press, 1984).

Irigaray, Luce. *Ce sexe qui ne'en est pas un* (Paris: Editions Minuit, 1977).

Jackson–Wilson, Anita and Sherry Borgers. "Disaffiliation Revisited." *Sex Roles* 28, No. 7/8(1993): 361–376.

Jameson, Frederic. *The Prison-House of Language* (Princeton: Princeton University Press, 1972).

———. "Architecture and the Critique of Ideology." In *The Ideologies of Theory, Essays 1971–1986, Volume 2, The Syntax of History* (Minneapolis: University of Minnesota Press, 1985).

Jencks, Christopher. *The Homeless* (Cambridge: Harvard University Press, 1994).

Johnson, Alice K. *Homelessness in America: A Historical and Contemporary Assessment* (St Louis, MO: Washington University Press, 1988).

Kasinitz, Philip. "Gentrification and Homelessness: The Single Room Occupant and the Inner City Revival. In *Urban and Social Change Review,* Special Issue on Homelessness, 17, No. 1 (1984): 9–14.

Kesey, Ken. *One Flew Over the Cuckoo's Nest* (New York: Viking, 1962).

Kopytoff, Igor. "The Cultural Biography of Things: Commoditization as a Process," In *The Social Life of Things,* edited by Arjun Appardurai (New York: Cambridge University Press, 1986).

Koven, Seth and Sonya Michel. *Mothers of a New World* (New York: Routledge, 1993).

Kozol, Johnathan. *Rachel and Her Children* (New York: Crown, 1988).

Laclau, Ernesto and Chantal Mouffe. *Hegemony and Socialist Strategy: Toward a Radical Democratic Politics* (London: Verso, 1985).

Lassalle, Yvonne. "We're not just Mothers, We're Women." Paper presented at the "Housing and the New World Order" conference, Allcraft Center, New York, June 1991.

119

LeCourbusier [Charles Edouard Jenneret]. *The City of Tomorrow* (1924, reprint Cambridge: The MIT Press, 1971).

————. *The Radiant City: Elements of a Doctrine of Urbanism to Be Used as the Basis of Our Machine–Age Civilization* (1933; reprint New York: Orion Press, 1967).

Lewis, Oscar. *La Vida: A Puerto Rican Family in the Culture of Poverty—San Juan and New York* (New York: Random House, 1966).

Liebow, Elliot. *Tally's Corner* (Boston: Little, Brown, 1967).

————. *Tell Them Who I Am* (New York: Free Press, 1993).

Longino, Helen. "Feminist Standpoint Theory and the Problems of Knowledge." *Signs* 19, No. 1(1993):201–12.

MacLoed, Jay. *Ain't No Makin' It: Leveled Aspirations in a Low-Income Neighborhood* (Boulder, CO: Westview Press, 1987).

Maier, Andrew. "The Homeless and the Post-Industrial City." *Political Geography Quarterly* 5 (1986):357–63.

Marcus, George and Michael Fischer. *Anthropology as Cultural Critique* (Chicago: University of Chicago Press, 1986).

Marcuse, Peter "Neutralizing Homelessness." *Socialist Review* 18 (1988):69–96.

Marin, Peter. "Born to Lose: The Prejudice Against Men" *The Nation,* Vol. 253, No. 2 (1991): 46–51.

Martinez-Alier, Verena (Stolcke). *Marriage, Class and Colour in 19th Century Cuba* (London: Cambridge University Press, 1974).

McCracken, Grant. "Homeyness: A Cultural Account of One Constellation of Consumer Goods and Meanings." In *Interpretive Consumer Research,* Association for Consumer Research (Provo, Utah: 1989).

Mitchell, J. Clyde. "The Components of Strong Ties among Homeless Women." *Social Networks* 9 (1987):37–47.

Moore, Henrietta. *A Passion for Difference: Essays in Athropology and Gender* (Bloomington: Indiana University Press, 1994).

National Coalition for the Homeless. *The International Right to Shelter* (Washington, D.C., 1989).

Newman, Katherine S. "Urban Anthropology and the Deindustrialization Paradigm." *Urban Anthropology* 14, Nos. 1–3 (1985):5–20.

New York City Open Space Task Force. *Open Space and the Future of New York: How to Analyze Community Open Space and Recreation Needs* (New York: Department of City Planning, 1988).

Partnership for the Homeless. "Assisting the Homeless in New York City: A Review of the Last Year and Challenge for 1988." (New York: Paternship for the Homeless, 1988).

Perin, Constance. *Belonging in America: Reading between the Lines* (Madison, WI: University of Wisconsin Press, 1988).

Piven, Frances Fox and Richard Cloward. *Regulating the Poor: The Functions of Public Welfare* (New York: Vintage, 1971).

120

Redburn, F. Stevens and Terry F. Buss. *Responding to America's Homeless: Public Policy Alternatives* (New York: Praeger, 1986).

Reich, Robert. *The Work of Nations: Preparing Ourselves for 21st-Century Capitalism* (New York: Alfred A. Knopf, 1991).

Reyes, Lilia M. and Laura D. Waxman. *A Status Report on Hunger and Homelessness in America's Cities: 1989* (Washington, D.C.: U.S. Conference of Mayors, 1989).

Rivlin, Leanne G. "A New Look at the Homeless." *Social Policy* 16, No.4 (1986):3–10.

Rix, Sara E., ed. *The American Woman, 1988–89 : A Report in Depth* (Washington, D.C.: Women's Research & Education Institute of the Congressional Caucus for Women's Issues, 1989).

Ropers, Richard H. *The Invisible Homeless: A New Urban Ecology* (New York: Human Sciences Press, 1988).

Rosler, Martha. *If You Lived Here: The City in Art, Theory and Social Activism* DIA Art Foundation Discussions in Contemporary Culture, edited by Brian Wallis, No. 6 (Seattle: Bay Press, 1991).

Rossi, Peter. *Down and Out in America: The Origins of Homelessness* (Chicago: University of Chicago Press, 1989).

Schneider, David M. "What is Kinship All About?" In *Kinship Studies in the Morgan Centential Year,* edited by Priscilla Reining (Washington, D.C.: The Anthropological Society of Washington, 1972).

Scheper-Hughes, Nancy. *Death Without Weeping* (Berkeley: University of California Press, 1992).

Schussheim, Morton J. *Housing Problems and Policies,* Congressional Research Service, Library of Congress (Washington, D.C.: 1987).

Schwede, Laurel and Matt T. Salo. "The Shelter Component of S-Night." Washington, D.C.: Center for Survery Methods Research, U.S. Department of Commerce, Bureau of the Census. Paper prepared for presentation at the Annual Research Conference, Arlington, Virginia, March 18, 1991.

Sennett, Richard. *The Conscience of the Eye: The Design and Social Life of Cities* (New York: Alfred A. Knopf, 1991).

Sidel, Ruth. "But Where are the Men?" In *Men's Lives,* edited by Michael Kimmel and Michael Messner (New York: MacMillan, 1992).

Sklar, Katherine Kish. "Historial Foundadtions of Women's Power." In *Mothers of a New World,* edited by Seth Koven and Sonya Michel (New York: Routledge, 1993).

Skockpol, Theda. *Protecting Soldiers and Mothers* (Cambridge: Cambridge University Press, 1992).

Smith, Carol A. "Race-Class-Gender Ideology in Guatemala: Modern and Anti-Modern Forms." *Comparative Studies in Society and History* 37(4): 723–749, October 1995.

Snow, David A. and Leon Anderson. *Down on Their Luck: A Study of Homeless Street People* (Berkeley: University of California Press, 1993).

Snow, David A., Susan Baker, Leon Anderson and Michael Martin. "The Myth of Pervasive Mental Illness among the Homeless." *Social Problems* 33, No. 5 (1986):407–423.

Solomon, Harry C. "The American Psychiatric Association in Relation to American Psychiatry." American Journal of Psychiatry 115 (1958):1–9.

Soja, Edward. *Postmodern Geographies: The Reassertion of Space in Critical Social Theory* (London: Verso, 1989).

Spradley, James. *You Owe Yourself a Drunk: An Ethnography of Urban Nomads* (Boston: Little, Brown, 1970).

Stack, Carol B. *All Our Kin: Strategies for Survival in a Black Community* (New York: Harper and Row, 1974).

Stanley, Liz. *Feminist Praxis: Research, Theory and Epistemology in Femininst Sociology* (London: Routledge, 1990).

Stolcke, Verena. "The naturalization of social inequality and women's subordination." In *Of Marriage and the Market,* edited by Kate Young, et. al. (London: Roultedge Kegan Paul, 1981)

Strauss, Claudia. "What Makes Tony Run? Schemas as Motives Reconsidered." In *Human Motives and Cultural Models,* edited by Roy D'Andrade and Claudia Strauss (Cambridge: Cambridge University Press, 1992).

Susser, Ida. *Norman Street: Poverty and Politics in an Urban Neighborhood* (New York: Oxford University Press, 1982).

Szasz, Thomas. *The Myth of Mental Illness: Foundations of a Theory of Personal Conduct* (New York: Hoeber-Harper, 1961).

Taeuber, Cynthia M. and Paul M. Siegel. *Counting the Nation's Homeless Population in the 1990 Census* (Washington, D.C.: U.S. Department of Commerce, Bureau of the Census, 1992).

Tafuri, Manfredo. *Architecture and Utopia: Design and Capitalist Development* (Cambridge: The MIT Press, 1973).

Torrey, E. Fuller. *Nowhere to Go: The Tragic Odyssey of the Homeless Mentally Ill* (New York: Harper and Row, 1988).

Trattner, Walter I. *From Poor Law to Welfare State* (New York: Free Press, 1979).

Trouillot, Michel–Rolph. *Haiti: State against Nation* (New York: Monthly Review Press, 1990).

U.S. Bureau of the Census. *1990 Census of Population, General Population Characteristics, New York* (Washington, D.C.: U.S. Department of Commerce, 1992).

U.S. Commission on Security and Cooperation In Europe. *Staff Report on Homelessness in the United States* (Washington, D.C., 1990)

U.S. Department of Housing and Urban Development. *A Report on Homeless Assistance Policy and Practice in the Nation's Five Largest Cities* (Washingtion, D.C.: 1989).

Urban Institiute. "Hunger and the Homeless: Poor Diets and Days Without Food." In *The Urban Institute Policy and Research Report* 18, No. 3 (1988):1–3.

Wach, Howard. "Unitarian Philanthropy and Cultural Hegemony in Comparative Perspective." *Journal of Social History* 26, No. 3 (1993): 539–57.

Wagner, David. *Checkerboard Square: Culture and Resistance in a Homeless Community* (Boulder, CO: Westview Press, 1993).

Wallace, R. "'Homelessness,' contagious destruction of housing, and municipal service cuts in New York City." *Environment and Planning* 21 (1989):1585–1603.

Watson, Sophie and Helen Austerberry. *Housing and Homelessness: A Feminist Perspective* (London: Routledge and Kegan Paul, 1986).

Weston, Kath. *Families We Choose: Lesbians, Gays, Kinship* (New York: Columbia University Press, 1992).

Williams, Brackette F. "The Public I/Eye: Conducting Fieldwork to do Homework on Homelessness in Two U.S. Cities." *Current Anthropology* 36, No. 1 (1995):1–51.

Willis, Paul. *Learning to Labour: How Working Class Kids Get Working Class Jobs* (Farnborough, UK: Saxon House, 1977).

Wittig, Monique. "The Mark of Gender." *Feminist Issues* 5, No. 2 (1985):3–12.

Wolch, Jennifer and Michael Dear. *Malign Neglect* (San Francisco: Jossey-Bass, 1993).

Wright, James D. "The Worthy and Unworthy Homeless." *Society* 25, no. 5 July/August (1988), pp. 64-69.

Wright, James D. and Eleanor Weber. *Homelessness and Health* (New York: McGraw-Hill, 1987).

123

INDEX